Jonah's Journey – A Tale of Two Minds

By Sharon A. Foster

"FROM A SPIRITUAL STANDPOINT, MOST MENTAL DISORDERS ARE A RESULT OF TRYING TO ESCAPE SOMETHING TRAUMATIC"

Dr. Bob Larson

JONAH'S JOURNEY – A TALE OF TWO MINDS

Copyright @2024 by Sharon A. Foster

All rights reserved. No part of this book may be reproduced or transmitted in any form or by any means without the written permission from the author.

Unless otherwise noted, all scriptures are from the KJV, English Standard Version, NIV and NKJV.

The author for emphasis had added some scripture underlining, italics or boldness, where needed.

ISBN: 9798321197264

This is a work of creative nonfiction. All of the events in this memoir are true to the best of the subject's memory. Some names and identifying features may have been changed to protect the identity of certain parties. The author, in no way endorses any company or brand depicted herein. The views expressed are solely those of the author.

TABLE OF CONTENTS

DEDICATION

FOREWORD BY VISHNU DHUNDA

ACKNOWLEDGEMENT

INTRODUCTION

PROLOGUE

CHAPTER 1 – WHERE EVENING FADE

CHAPTER 2 – TERROR BY NIGHT

CHAPTER 3 – WHERE MORNING DAWNS

CHAPTER 4 – BEFORE YOU WERE BORN

CHAPTER 5 – SINCE MY YOUTH

CHAPTER 6 – TROUBLES, MANY AND BITTER

CHAPTER 7 – FOWLER'S SNARE

CHAPTER 8 – THE FIRE

CHAPTER 9 – FIERY TRIALS

CHAPTER 10 – JUSTICE LIKE WATER

CHAPTER 11 – LIKE COLD WATER

CHAPTER 12 – PURE WATER

CHAPTER 13 – ROCK OF MY REFUGE

CHAPTER 14 – WAVER BETWEEN TWO

CHAPTER 15 – HE RESTORES MY SOUL

CHAPTER 16 – BE ZEALOUS AND REPENT

CHAPTER 17 – HE THAT DWELLS

CHAPTER 18 – WE DO NOT WRESTLE AGAINST FLESH AND BLOOD

CHAPTER 19 – HIS UNFAILING LOVE

CHAPTER 20 – THE SECRET PLACE

CHAPTER 21 – NOT BY MIGHT, NOR BY POWER BUT BY HIS SPIRIT

CHAPTER 22 – MY TREASURE, MY BRIDE

CHAPTER 23 – KEEP HIM ALIVE

CHAPTER 24 – CRUEL AS THE GRAVE

CHAPTER 25 – CRUSHED IN SPIRIT

CHAPTER 26 – HEALING IN HIS WINGS

CHAPTER 27 – STOLEN WATER IS SWEET

CHAPTER 28 – STAND AT THE CROSSROADS

CHAPTER 29 – YOUR MOTHER'S INSTRUCTIONS

CHAPTER 30 – MORE THAN YOU CAN CHEW

CHAPTER 31 – YOUR OWN WICKEDNESS

CHAPTER 32 – MANY ARE THE AFFLICTIONS

CHAPTER 33 – MY SOUL FINDS REST

CHAPTER 34 – WHEN THE TIME IS RIGHT

CHAPTER 35 – HE WHO FINDS A WIFE

CHAPTER 36 – THE HEART OF STONE

CHAPTER 37 – A COMPANION OF FOOLS

CHAPTER 38 – DARKENED IN THEIR UNDERSTANDING

CHAPTER 39 – THE PRESENCE OF GOD

EPILOGUE

GLOSSARY OF TERMS

DEDICATION

I dedicate this book, my life story to Jesus Christ, as it is ONLY through His Saving Grace that I am alive today to tell the tale. He never let me go, even in the midst of running and hiding from His purpose and plan for my life. He never gave up on me and for this I am forever thankful and grateful.

To my adoring wife, who despite the harrowing pain I brought into our lives, persevered and pleaded for my life and salvation. She devoted years to fasting and prayer so that I could be counted among the true redeemed of the Lord.

I dedicate this book to all Standers and Runners everywhere.

"Look at what the Lord has done!!"

"Therefore, the redeemed of the LORD shall return, and come with singing unto Zion; and everlasting joy shall be upon their head: they shall obtain gladness and joy; and sorrow and mourning shall flee away"

ISAIAH 51:11

FOREWORD

By
VISHNU DHUNDA

My journey with the subject of this memoir, my dear childhood friend, who I have personally known for all of his life, to showcase how his story unfolded is nothing short of a miracle. To say that God came through for him in so many ways, is a testament to myself, and many others associated with this remarkable tale; of the relentless, and persuasive love of a Savior, who will leave the 99 already secured in His care to pursue that 1 lost sheep.

Jonah was not merely lost, but was in flagrant rebellion, as time after time, he rejected God and the calling that was evident on his life. His mother, may her dear soul, rest in peace, proclaimed to everyone that her son is a "man of God", even when his ungodly lifestyle screamed the contrary of such faith filled declarations.

His many near-death experiences, only momentarily led him back to the Savior, but each time he sought sanctuary in God, it was always short-lived, and the lure and lust of the world will capture him in its tangled web once more!!

Today, I can say with the blessed assurance that he has finally come back home to his Father and has found the peace that the world, that he kept running towards, was incapable of giving him. He was running towards something unattainable apart from Christ, as he has found out the hard way, that a life lived without Christ is a crisis. Any life without Jesus is vain, useless and worthless. There exists no true prosperity, peace or joy without Jesus Christ. Praise the Lord that Jonah is now free indeed.... the prayers of his righteous mother; and subsequently his kingdom wife, Sharon; have finally been answered.

Shalom and Blessings

Vishnu "Lovey" Dhunda

ACKNOWLEDGEMENTS

All praise and glory to my Lord and Savior, Yeshua Hamashiach, The Great God, The Almighty God and the Holy Spirit who teaches, leads and guides.

My parents, Albert and Girlie; my siblings, from my mother and father and half siblings from my father's side.

My friends and family from my hometown of Mafeking Village, Mayaro, as well as Gasparillo, Tableland and Cunupia.

My first pastor, who is now deceased, Rev. Khan

My mother's close friend, Mrs. Margaret Greer, who was a constant source of strength for my mother and our family unit.

My childhood friend, Vishnu 'Lovey' Dhunda.

Pastor Chanel Price, for consistently standing in the gap with my wife, as a mentor to her; the *Clubhouse* meet up warriors; Pastor Valecia Carey, Eric Smith, Kimbri Johnson, Joanne Garceron, Julie Allsup, and those who faithfully held my wife's hands in prayer and supplication for my salvation; Carmen Mata, Priya Joseph Pereira, Sharifa Neille-Kwao and Jackie Morgan. RPMTPMinistry, founder and C.E.O. Mrs. Keshia Torruella.

The lone warrior in Trinidad, the anointed and powerful woman of God, Ms. Theresa Charles, who battled alongside my dear wife, when the heat was too intense!

PC Celestine Badge number 21121 and WPC Singh Badge number 19030.

Rev. Earl Sampson, who renewed our vows on the 24th September, 2022 at our home as a thanksgiving service as well, and re-baptized my wife and I on the shores of Mayaro; the exact beach where we originally stood before God and man on the 25th April 2010, pledging our commitment to each other.

Dr. Kendra Phillips and Natalie Morales-Thomas for sacrificially proofreading the manuscript and ensuring it was ready for the publishers. Your invaluable services are deeply appreciated! Thank you both!!

Everyone who ever said a genuine prayer over my life or had any connection with me. I sincerely thank you all!!

"No mortal can fully comprehend the efficacy of prayer. We need a revelation of intercession. It is the only hope for humanity."

Morton Bustard

INTRODUCTION

"It is pointless to embark on any journey if you do not believe yourself worthy of the destination"

Anthon St. Maarten

I share my testimony, boldly and unashamedly to everyone, wherever I go. The joy of the Lord is truly my strength.

People may wonder why am I so zealous for God and the love of the Holy Spirit? I vividly recall numerous life-changing experiences in God's Holy presence, and have been aware of Him for most of my life.

At times, my radical enthusiasm may seem insane to those who do not understand my passion for Christ. I long to witness His Glory visit us as the Book of Acts reveals.

I am not ashamed of my humble beginnings; as my story gives God glory.

I am no longer that person. The old man is dead, and today I am alive only because of the mercy and grace of God.

Mercy said, "NO!"

It's been almost two years since my fifth, and most fatal, near-death experience that shifted my life forever. Despite being raised in a religious background, I chose to walk a dark, eerie path away from God, making many unwise and ungodly decisions. Were it not for a praying mother and wife, I would not be here in the Land of the Living.

On many such occasions, I struggled with my identity, torn between two minds and two masters. I professed to love God, yet lived as the biggest sinner this side of Trinidad and Tobago, causing immense agony and anguish to my wife, the author of this memoir.

My reckless lifestyle placed me in numerous life-threatening situations, yet the relentless, stubborn love of our Heavenly Father never ceased pursuing me.

Throughout this journey, I faced demonic attacks, satanic encounters, and witnessed witchcraft performances. It was only through a series of divine encounters, supernatural favor, and heavenly miracles, signs and wonders that I was saved from the bowels of hell.

Many prophetic words were spoken over me at various points in my life, and I rejected every one of them as I ran away in rebellion.

Within the pages of this book lies a true story that may seem improbable, but with God on my side, I conquered and slew every Goliath as God arose in me; the David that I was born to be.

A man after His own heart.

PROLOGUE

Forged from the loins of Albert and Girlie Foster in a tiny, remote fishing village called Mafeking, came forth the birth of this prized son, where addiction and abuse were his constant companions. His very existence, from inception, was in a constant spiritual battle as the forces of darkness sought to eradicate the purpose that was balled into his divine destiny.

This son, destined for greatness as the mantle of God rested mightily upon his life despite many near-death experiences assigned to steal, kill and destroy him, fell as every fiery dart was quenched by the apparent wall of fire that hedged him in preservation.

As he walked through the trenches of life, he arose out of destitution through multiple favors and doors that were supernaturally and miraculously opened for him by the Hand of God.

Out of this meteoric rise from poverty to glory, tragic backlashes from the enemy plaguing him with sickness, witchcraft, abuse and a wrongful diagnosis of mental ill-health.

God's predestined plans for this special, anointed man after His own heart manifested after many years when he was saved from death, yet again. However, this time marked by a tragic turn of supernatural events included excessive bleeding that almost spilled all his life force unto the ground. In fact, the jaws of death savagely gripped him while simultaneously escorting him into a Christless eternity.

BUT....

God's transformative power visited and resurrected him on that hospital bed in the wee hours on the 31st of July 2022.

God restored his life!

His purpose!

His destiny!

His marriage......

CHAPTER ONE
WHERE EVENING FADES

PSALM 65:8(b)

.... where evening fades.... you call forth songs of joy...

31st JULY 1965

Girlie braced herself for the worst – an onslaught of verbal abuse and the inevitable beating that would follow. She glanced at their young daughter Cindy, who was busy scribbling away at a scrap of paper that she found lying around and wondered how lost she was in her three-year-old little world; that maybe she was impervious to the relentless calamity storming around her innocent mind.

Albert screamed at his wife, beside himself with fury, that she had not finished cooking his dinner. It was just one of those days, as she was now into her third month of pregnancy, and receiving all the signs and symptoms that plagued her since she discovered her impregnation. She had a rough day, but tried to get his meal ready before he came home from work. She knew her intoxicated husband's abuse and cruelty increased when his food was not on time! She estimated the timing, as she sought to ensure that Albert's dinner would be hot and ready when he arrived home.

Father, just help his anger. God, I love him but he is such a beast when he is drunk and hungry.

She pleaded, "Honey, I am so sorry, but I felt extremely unwell. I cannot understand it, but it was a horrible day for me. This pregnancy is much more difficult than my last one, so just give me another half an hour and I will have your dinner ready, okay?"

Albert, turned beet red in anger. "What foolishness you are saying woman?" he bellowed. "You think my day was peachy? That d*** boss of mine had me driving up and down the entire sloppy, dangerous hillside trying to navigate my way through those trees and rocks. Almost had me killed! I had to stop by the bar to have a few shots just to clear my head" He grunted as he relived the ordeal.

"Now, for me to come home, hungry and exhausted and you not have my food ready, is unacceptable. You wasted an entire day, while I slave for you, and this is my thanks?"

He slapped her with the back of his hand and she felt her ear ring.

Cindy, looked on with a dazed expression in her eyes; most likely thinking that this type of behavior was acceptable between mommies and daddies.

"I am fed up of you, blasted lazy woman! You do nothing, but give me a hard time! You can't even get a job to help yourself! Why did I ever marry an illiterate b**** who can't read nor write is beyond me.'

Girlie grew more fearful, as she watched him scamper around, seemingly looking for something.

"Albert, please," she pleaded, "I am so sorry. This won't happen again. Please just calm down. I will try to hurry and speed it up so you can eat..."

She was unable to finish her pleas for mercy as he flipped the table over, scattering all the ingredients that were prepared for the completion of the meal.

Her eyes widened in horror! Accustomed to his brutality, she vaguely sensed this erratic behavior was new and untested. She continued watching him, as he ransacked all the seasonings and condiments that laid ready for the preparation of his evening meal. He grabbed a nearby bucket, and proceeded to scope its freezing contents out of the big barrel used to keep their water supplies, as they had no indoor plumbing.

Albert charged toward her as she stood helplessly rooted to the floor. He splashed the entire contents of the bucket over her head. The icy-cold water engulfed her entire being, as a sickening stirring grabbed hold of her stomach, knotting it, where her precious baby lay. Alfred then began beating her with the empty bucket.

Blood-curdling screams echoed throughout the little fishing village, as their young daughter witnessed her mother being viciously attacked in a manner that bordered on sadism.

Girlie managed to grab their daughter and ran towards the nearby bushes, hoping to find refuge within their thorny sanctuary. She ran and ran as his angry commands grew faint.

Finally reaching a huge, mango tree, Girlie, panting and out of breath, sat under it as the evening faded into streaks of moonlit rays. She quieted the sobs of her now distraught daughter, beginning to sing to her to make a joyful noise in spite of this horrendous turn of events.

"Yes, Jesus loves me, yes, Jesus loves me.

Yes, Jesus loves me.

The Bible tells me so"

CHAPTER TWO
TERROR BY NIGHT

Psalm 91:5

Do not be afraid of the terror by night....

Despite the horrific events, Girlie continued singing to her daughter, even as she could faintly hear Albert's bellowing command for her to come back.

Amidst Cindy's distress, Girlie also had to deal with the biting of the night air, further exacerbated by the wet clothes that clung to her frail, trembling frame. The shooting pain in the pit of her stomach that held her baby magnified. She mindfully covered her stomach with her hands with an inner knowing that there was something very special about this baby. This baby, who from the beginning of its conception had placed an added burden on her tiny frame; her body, that now bore indelible marks and scars associated with the endless beatings from her husband. Albert, a man who was once her knight in shining armor, had now transformed into a beast in a human's body.

Cindy was scared. As the darkness grew, so did her anxiety. The screech of the nocturnal animals was echoed in surround sound. Insistently, Girlie pleaded to her Father, to shield them from the terrors of the night. She swore she heard the leers of every night creature right on her shoulders. Owls, bats and moths flew eerily around their scared, frozen mother-daughter bodies.

Jesus, be our shelter. Our shield and buckler. Our fortress and High Tower. Lord, in You alone I place my trust.

I will trust and not be afraid.

I will not be afraid of the terrors of the night!!

Girlie tried comforting her overwrought child, while trying to dispel her own fears by quoting scriptures. Despite her inability to read or write, she memorized certain parts of scriptures and inscribed them on the walls of her heart. Though her knowledge of the Bible was limited, she relied on the promptings and leading of the Holy Spirit. He was a constant Lamp unto her feet and the Light unto her path.

She recoiled in fear as a snake slithered toward them. Her heart pounded loudly as she watched its impending arrival with trepidation.

She closed her eyes and immediately recited the scriptures that proclaimed that snakes and scorpions shall be trampled upon. With full awareness that the scriptures meant spiritual snakes and scorpions, Girlie knew that the power of God could keep her and her daughter from even the physical manifestation of imminent dangers from such night creatures.

Girlie immediately began praying under her breath, as God promised in His Word that nothing shall harm her, especially as she was seeking refuge from the villainous brute that Albert had become. His uncontrollable temper and excessive drinking caused endless chaos and contention in their home. A home that she yearned to make into a haven with her little family. Steamy tears streamed down her frozen cheeks.

As she reopened her eyes, she no longer saw the serpent that was ominously approaching them, just moments ago.

She sighed in relief and praise.

The Angel of the Lord encamps round about those who fear the Lord!

Just then, her eyes almost bulged out of its sockets, as she saw the fiery ball of flame, the 'soucouyant' flying in the night sky. The village oldest woman, Miss Meena, infamously known for her shape-shifting abilities, was out in the terror of the night, searching for her next blood victim.

Father, make me invisible to every evil force that is out preying, tonight.

The grace and strength of the Father fell mightily upon her, as a great peace flooded her soul.

Thankfully, her daughter fell asleep on her lap, but Girlie was growing apprehensive, as the night wind blew on her now almost dried clothes. The bitterly cold water thrown on her earlier caused her grave discomfort as she shivered in the chilling night air.

The whistle of the wind brought with it, a surge of mosquitoes and bugs that were hell-bent on making them their snack.

She appealed to heaven, again to dispatch mighty angels to keep her from this noisome pestilence.

"Lord, please cover us under the shadow of your wings. Lord, may we be sheltered under your mighty outstretched arms!" She muttered feebly, as overwhelmed with grief, and the shock of the events of the night, she finally drifted off to sleep.

CHAPTER THREE
WHERE MORNING DAWNS

Psalms 65:8 (a)

The whole earth is filled with awe at your wonders; where morning dawns....

Girlie, was startled awake by the chirping of the birds and extreme bodily pains: partially caused by the hard bark of the tree against her back; which she had managed to prop herself against throughout the night, as well as the barbarous blows dealt by her errant husband last night.

She shuddered in remembrance.

Cindy slept peacefully on her lap, oblivious to the terror and dangers of the surroundings. Though darkness still embraced them, Girlie knew that dawn was swiftly approaching, as she heard the distant crowing of the chickens that she farmed.

"It's time to face whatever lies before me,' she said softly.

"This is the day that the Lord has made. I will rejoice and be glad in this day!" she weaponized, counterattacking fear with faith!

Girlie woke up her sleeping child and began her trek to the home that she tried so desperately to make a peaceful and comfortable one for Albert and their daughter.

Albert was such a wonderful person when sober, but his insatiable desire to excessively consume alcohol was mind-boggling.

Girlie tried to be a good and perfect housewife. Never rude, always respectful, loving and kind to this man that she loved so passionately.

Through her weekly studies, Girlie learned what the Bible said about being submissive to her own husband, and as much as possible, did exactly what was required of her, as a helpmeet suitable for her husband. Yet, when he came home drunk and disorderly, it was hell on earth as his fury raged like a consuming fire, destroying anything and everything in his path.

Reluctantly, she climbed the stairs to their humble home, mostly made of wood and some concrete. She cherished their family's dwelling as it represented the hard work and sacrifices her husband made for them to possess their own home, instead of wasting money on rent or seeking abode in a relative's house.

She tucked Cindy into bed, and ventured into the kitchen, ignoring the nagging pains felt all over her battered body. Her husband was nowhere in the house. Afraid to even search him out, Girlie began cleaning up the mess that he had made the previous evening.

The fragrant aroma of freshly brewed coffee, cooked eggs from her chickens, and the baking of homemade bread filled the house. It truly represented the perfect setting of the "Proverbs

31" woman who takes care of her household. Unfortunately, no matter how Girlie tried, keeping her husband happy seemed to be an unattainable feat.

Cindy was ravenously devouring her breakfast, when Albert appeared in the doorway. She dropped her spoon in fright, but her father was smiling.

"Good morning, my babies!" he exclaimed enthusiastically, as he lovingly caressed his wife's stomach, planting a kiss on her bruised lips and Cindy's forehead.

"Good morning", they said in unison, keenly aware by now that this was the good side of Albert. Loving, gracious and ever so kind despite the previous night's gruesome episode.

Life would indeed be blissful, if this was the consistent side of him. However, one episode of drinking changed him into a walking demon that everyone, even the people in the village, was scared of. His ghastly behavior terrorized all, both young and old.

"This coffee is so good!" he enthused. "Sweetheart, you outdid yourself this morning. I think this is the best tasting brew you have ever made!"

She smiled, though still very much shaken by last evening's events.

"Tell me something. How the heck did I end up on the hammock downstairs?" he queried with furrowed brows.

Girlie had no clue of how to respond. How could she remind him of the events that transpired and not rouse any unnecessary drama, especially while he was in such a terrific mood?

"Well, honey, you were so tired from your day, that you passed out on the hammock, without even eating your dinner", she offered, not wanting to lie, but also not desiring to reveal the true nature of events from the past evening.

Her body, though aflame with pain, and being in her first trimester, couldn't take any strong pain medication. At that very moment, she longed for bed, the weariness crashing down on her entire mind and body.

"Oh, yes my day was terrible, one of the worst days of my life," he recalled. "I am hoping for a better day, today. Say a prayer for me, will you, my love? To your invisible friend from another planet," he joked. That was one of her pet peeves; his open mockery of her faith.

She hated it.

She knew her Lord and Savior as real and personal, always present in her time of need.

Girlie simply nodded.

Yes, she would definitely be praying. She desperately desired him to have a good work day so there wouldn't be a repeat of what happened the night before.

As Girlie cleaned up after everyone, she sang....

'Tis so sweet to trust in Jesus

Just to take Him at His Word,

Just to rest upon His promise

Just to know, "Thus saith the Lord."

CHAPTER FOUR
BEFORE YOU WERE BORN

Jeremiah 1:5

Before I formed you in the womb, I knew you; before you were born, I sanctified you; and I ordained you as a prophet to the nation.

SUNDAY 19TH DECEMBER 1965

Girlie barely had enough breath to call out to her neighbor next door to fetch the village midwife, and to carry Cindy over to her best friend, Margaret's house.

What started off as brief, fleeting pain soon intensified into true birth pangs.

This baby was not due yet, not for another few weeks, but he seemed determined to make his grand entrance sooner rather than later. She had just celebrated her 24th birthday on the 11th, and mused that if he wanted to come early, why not on that day?

Lord knows she already felt such a connection to this baby, such a love that was unfathomable. So intense. So protective. What better way for them to also share the same birthday!

She screamed in agony, as another bout of pain ripped through her frame.

Lord, let this midwife come quickly! This child is in a hurry to get here!

Jonah made his grand entrance at 8:15 that night.

After eight hours of tormenting agony, he finally crowned his way out of the comfort of his mother's womb, to come forth into this new world.

The midwife instantly recognized something was wrong. He was incredibly yellow. Too yellow! An acute form of jaundice. The newborn, barely breathing, his chest restricted and congested. He needed immediate medical attention.

Girlie was beside herself.

"Is he okay?"

The joy she felt at the birth of a son, totally short-lived.

A SON! She wanted to give her husband a boy child, to carry on his name, and her prayers were answered, and now this?

She immediately began to pray! Interceding for this new life that already was being taken away. His young life, already threatened by the jaws of death.

No way!

He must live, and fulfill the calling of God upon His life!

She began wailing, as the midwife bundled him to be carried to the nearby local health facility, thankfully, only five minutes away.

Albert was working late, so she very much doubted that he had heard the news that she went into premature labor. He usually did not work on a Sunday, but his boss needed the extra hand, and they needed the extra money, so he reluctantly reported into work.

She could surely use his comforting arms right now! Overwhelming sorrow began draping over her as the severity of the baby's predicament loomed before her.

As the midwife's assistants continued tidying her, attempting to make her comfortable after her ordeal, her husband burst through the doors!

Fresh tears flowed freely as he gathered her in his arms. He kissed her and assured her that everything will be alright.

She sobbed into his shoulder as Albert held her. His own sorrow mirroring hers, they both held on to hope that their precious little baby's life would be spared.

Christmas day was marred by Jonah's hospitalization who was still in the ICU fighting for his life. Albert and Girlie tried to make it as special as possible for Cindy, who could not understand why her baby brother was not at home to celebrate with them. With her father not drinking as much, their home was less chaotic than usual. However, the somberness was tangible and made the atmosphere thick with grief.

Her mother, seemingly so frail and distraught, could be heard crying out on her knees for her brother's life to be saved. Cindy's mind questioned how her new brother was in danger and from what he needed to be rescued. Rescued from what? And who? Her parents' preoccupation with Jonah, caused Cindy to feel confused and neglected.

Her mother's incessant cries filled the home as day after day, it appeared that Jonah would indeed die. As with each passing day, brought very little hope of him making this out alive, Jonah's tiny underdeveloped body was overwhelmed with bronchitis and jaundice.

At this point only an absolute miracle can save Jonah.

Thankfully...

MIRACLES ARE GOD'S SPECIALITY!

CHAPTER FIVE
SINCE MY YOUTH

Psalm 71:5 to 6

For you have been my hope, SOVEREIGN LORD, my confidence since my youth. From birth I have relied on you; you brought me forth from my mother's womb. I will ever praise you.

Jonah miraculously made it through the worst. After two grueling months, he was discharged from the hospital. Girlie became obsessed with his health and well-being. Though he was out of immediate danger, he was frail and needed meticulous care.

Due to the attention given to Jonah, Cindy felt ignored and grew very resentful toward her baby brother. In her innocence, she did not understand the laser-like focus on Jonah. Furthermore, her father's drinking increased and so did the beatings to her mother. Girlie periodically ran away to stay at relatives' homes, but with no source of income and now two babies, that was not a sustainable solution.

Albert would humbly apologize and petition for Girlie to give him another chance at being a better husband and father. Of course, the Christian thing for her to do was to forgive him and try again, even though she was growing increasingly tired of the atrocities he dished out almost weekly now.

By March of 1967, she found out that she was pregnant again. She felt bittersweet about it. She loved children and wanted as many as the Lord would allow; however, her husband exhibited no signs of change and she knew that this did not create a healthy environment in which to raise her children. To add another child to the mix just did not seem right. But her trust in God took precedence over everything else.

She said, like Mary, "be it unto me according to your word, my Lord."

Unlike Jonah's, this pregnancy was without much incident and a welcome relief to her. She gave birth to a very feisty, healthy boy on the 1st of October that year. Girlie felt blessed to have another boy, and her husband was over the moon, now with a pair of sons to carry on his name.

Maybe now, Albert would realize that he needed to serve as a better example for his sons and change his demonic ways and lifestyle, she mused. The drinking and violence that Albert displayed almost weekly had subsided, and there was relative peace and calm after the birth of Roland. Girlie was ecstatic! God had finally answered her prayers as Albert became the man, she knew he could be.

Girlie found joy in caring for her family, and even found a way to create income by catering for school and neighborhood events. She carried the children to church every Sunday with her, whilst her husband stayed at home.

Albert still claimed no belief in "her friend from another planet" and Girlie dealt with that in prayer, rather than arguing about it for fear of resurrecting the old Albert again.

Unfortunately, Jonah's health deteriorated once more. Girlie found herself taking him almost weekly to the health centers and "herbalist doctors." Jonah, thin and fragile, barely ate. He was forbidden to go outside to play, confined to the safety of the walls of his home. Often seen peeking through the windows, Jonah looked at the games the village children were having outside, the excitement and fun, the sheer joy of camaraderie and friendship. He repeatedly asked his mother to join in with them. Girlie's heart broke every time she replied "no" to him.

Girlie's obsession with Jonah was keenly noticed by Cindy who still felt very much alone and neglected. Albert, too, seemed to favor his boys, and hardly paid her any attention or affection. Girlie, though loving and kind to all her children, always cherished Jonah more than her and Roland.

Girlie cried out to God for Jonah's total healing. She relied on the goodness and grace of God for Jonah. She knew that the difficulty she went through in her pregnancy and even the ongoing health challenges with him, were indicative of a greater purpose. He was a special child to God. Satan's pursuit seemed relentless upon his life.

At one point, delicate four-year-old Jonah, awoke from his sleep, congested and barely breathing, almost blue from a lack of oxygen. Girlie, in panic and desperation upon realizing that thick mucus clogged his airway passages inhibiting his breathing, had to use her mouth as a sucking agent to dispel the mucus plug from his nostrils. It was a rollercoaster for Girlie; who wanted nothing more than her first-born son to be totally healed and delivered. Her faith in God accepted and expected nothing less than this miracle.

CHAPTER SIX
TROUBLES, MANY AND BITTER

PSALMS 71:20(NIV)

Though you have made me see troubles, many and bitter, you will restore my life again; from the depths you will again bring me up.

Trouble never seemed to elude the Foster's. One day, while the children were in school, Albert ran up the stairs in a panic. He was sweating profusely and appeared to have been in a fight.

"What happened?", Girlie whimpered in anguish. "Did something happen at work?" She continued in sheer panic.

"My boss, that old dirty dog, has accused me of stealing money from the register. He didn't even ask, he SAID it was me".

"After all my years of loyal service to this ***hole, he thinks that I, of all people, would do this to him!! I am sure it was his wife, as she was there earlier, but he felt insulted and said his wife will never do that to him!" he bellowed in anger.

"I may be many things, but a thief, never, I will chop off any hands I find stealing. I loathe stealing! You saw what happened when my nephew, Michael, came here and stole Jonah's silver coins. That beating I gave him, bet he will never, ever think of doing that foolishness ever again in life," he boasted.

Girlie was horrified by this sudden turn of events. Things were wonderful in their household. Everything was running so smoothly. Jonah was now eight years old, and seemed to have outgrown the condition of jaundice, plus his bouts with bronchitis and asthma were diminishing as he grew older. He was becoming a healthy and vibrant young boy. Very intelligent and the head of his class. Likable, relatable and extremely talkative. Girlie knew it was nothing short of the miraculous power of Almighty God in full operation on their lives.

Now this.

What does this mean?

Cindy was at a crucial stage now, where she was just about to enter high school.

Albert continued his ranting, "I did not take that too lightly, I let that fool have it. I beat the crap out of him!"

"You beat him up?" Girlie asked with widened eyes.

"Yes, I picked up a 2x4 piece of lumber and was just so enraged that he was branding me as something I hate – I let him have it".

He stared at her.

She looked back at him, not believing her ears.

"Albert, sweetheart, you can go to jail" she lamented. "You beat him with a piece of wood!

Is he dead?" she screeched as the implications of it dawned upon her! A look of total horror washed over Albert. He fell on his knees before her. Visibly shaken at what she just revealed.

"Oh my God! I am not sure. He just slumped to the floor, but he was still breathing."

He panicked, becoming delirious.

"I can't go to jail! What will happen to you and the children?" he sobbed while she held him.

Girlie began crying out to God. She always knew Albert's anger would one day get him into trouble.

"We will figure this out. God will make a way of escape for us, my love."

She offered him words of love and encouragement as Albert verbally recalled the horror of his hasty actions.

Proverbs 14:17

"A quick-tempered person does foolish things, and the one who devises evil schemes is hated."

Girlie recalled that scripture and its application to this situation, this trouble that erupted from nowhere! She again had to rely on the power of her Father because this seemed like an impossible situation. The police will be upon them at any moment with questions and to possibly arrest her husband for either murder or attempted murder/manslaughter, whichever one was applicable based on the state of his boss.

Albert went to lay down while she prayed and went about her daily chores. The children came home from school and were happy to see their father at home. Jonah especially, as he laid on his father's lap all afternoon, telling him of his day at school. Jonah loved talking, engaging in conversations every moment he got.

Later that evening, word came to them that Albert's boss was assaulted by possible bandits, and was taken to the hospital; having amnesia and severe fractures as a result of the beating he endured.

He somehow recalled to the police that money was missing, but apart from that, his memory was blank.

Albert was shocked at this turn of events.

Maybe this God that his wife always prayed to, might somehow be real?

CHAPTER SEVEN
FOWLER'S SNARE

Psalms 91:3

'Surely, He will save you from the Fowler's snare....

Albert started drinking heavily again. Ever since that episode with his boss, he became depressed and was incapable of keeping a job for more than a couple of weeks. With the drinking, came his uncontrollable anger that wreaked havoc on their family life once more. The few years of peace after his second son was born, now just a distant memory, decimated to more brutality than ever before. Except now, the children too fell in the path of Albert Foster's unleashed fury.

Many times, Girlie would take the blows meant for her children, as she stood as a barrier between them and their father's wrath. The children's lives were now disrupted with Albert's temper, as he somehow could not rid himself of the internal demons that terrorized him. The more he sought solace in the bottle, the more the evil overtook him.

Albert was supposed to have given his life over to the Lord, after God miraculously displaced him from the hot water that his unbridled anger placed him in, but now he turned to the wrong spirit, one that was barreling him down the rocky road of destruction. An evil cycle that seemed to have sucked him into their hell.

Girlie made several pleas to the various authorities to assist her husband, but Albert became so unbearable and unlikeable in the small fishing village of Mafeking that all they offered was pity for her and the children, along with the grim warning to leave him before something fatal happened.

How could she do that? She had three children and no viable income. Whatever little savings they had was either spent because of his inability to keep a job, or used by him to fund his drinking and smoking habits.

Albert needed help desperately. And this time, she felt as if nothing was helping. It seemed he was given over to a reprobate mind.

Albert, delivered from the fowler's snare before, seemed to be even further entrapped by the devil's plan to steal, kill and ultimately destroy him.

One day during the summer vacation, Albert took his two sons on a hunting expedition. A dangerous journey that almost got them killed. The boys were incapable of handling the handmade guns that were used which resulted in Roland almost shooting his brother, and Jonah almost killing himself and his father.

Another time, Albert took them fishing, with sharpened knives in their hands, resulting in several cuts from their ill-fated adventure.

Not too long after that incident, he took them to see "Aunty Carol," a name the boys found odd because they could not remember having an aunt by that name.

Albert's erratic behavior was becoming increasingly alarming. As with each passing year, things only grew worst.

News reached Girlie that Albert had carried the boys off to a deep, dark part of the countryside to visit an "obeah" man who had a "buck." On their return from that trip, Jonah became pensive and moody, not the same child that everyone dubbed "SUNSHINE." Girlie asked her son what could have traumatized him like that, but to no avail. She dared not ask Albert, trying to avoid another beating.

At another point, Albert took Jonah to work with him and allowed him to drive the tractor through the forest, all by himself, endangering his life, yet again! Albert grew more and more careless and reckless with their sons. Girlie became increasingly concerned that he was not portraying a good "fatherly" image for the boys. His drinking, smoking and womanizing ways were setting a destructive example.

She persisted in raising God-fearing soldiers for God's army! Praying fervently against those harmful habits for her sons. However, her husband's brutality towards them seemed unabated. With no end in sight, Girlie tried many times to leave, but each time she had to run right back home, as the benevolence of her family and friends were relatively short-term.

Girlie's mental state was becoming unhinged.

CHAPTER EIGHT
THE FIRE

Psalms 21:9(b)

"...the Lord shall swallow them up in His wrath, and the fire shall devour them"

Girlie was inconsolable. She was beaten mercilessly yet again by her husband, another episode of his sheer anger and madness, visibly displayed before their children. Jonah stood and looked on with a dark, evil look in his eyes. Cindy was transfixed, too numb to say a word. Roland was crying for him to stop beating "mammy!"

Jonah was increasingly reticent with each passing day, almost unrecognizable to his mother. Once a loving and obedient child, he started to become "hardened".

Girlie cried out to the Lord for this to finally come to an end. She began questioning if he had turned His Face away as He saw the suffering endured, and yet no respite was in sight. The children went off to school, despite the horrific incident that they had just witnessed. Their grades were severely suffering because of the internal turmoil at home.

Albert, too, left for probably the 100th job that he tried holding on to, since that fiasco two years ago with his boss... with a sinister promise to her to finish what he started.

He will surely kill me.

"To finish what he started," sounded more like a death sentence to her. Barely able to breathe, she was sure she had some cracked ribs from all the buffeting and kicks she received at the once-loving hands of her dear Albert. The man who promised to love and cherish her... the man who swept her off her feet away from her mother's home.

She was only too happy to get away from that hell hole anyway. Unable to pursue an education like her other siblings, she was treated as a slave for everyone.

She was the last of six, and oddly enough physically different to them. Girlie, dark-skinned with curly hair, was in stark contrast to her light-skinned, straight-haired sisters and brothers. There were talks in the village of her true paternity. Girlie was ostracized and never given equal opportunities like the rest; hence her inability to read nor write.

She dialed her friend Margaret's number to assist her in getting medical attention.

Girlie received very strong pain medication which left her feeling extremely groggy and delirious. The children returned home from school, and on seeing their mom's condition, grew anxious with concern.

Cindy hastily began to prepare supper, as she knew from experience, that her father wanted his dinner when he returned home from a hard day's work. He would not care by what means. The sun was extremely fiery, and with him out all day working, his mood will surely match the scorching heat of its rays.

Albert was unreasonable and callous. Though he was beastly before Roland was born, with a few peaceful years in between, it was not until after he left his job with his boss who eventually became a "vegetable" because of his injuries after being "robbed", that her father was never the same. In fact, the past two years were the toughest.

Very little food to eat, relentless beatings and no money, not even for Sunday afternoon treats, for which they always had a few dollars to spare for those anticipated outings; now made life unbearable. Cindy could not help but think that when the boys came, her parents changed drastically, as their dad was always drunk and their mother doted on her brothers, especially her stupid brother, Jonah. Cindy disliked him immensely. She felt like a second-class citizen to her brothers. And yet she had to cook and help her mother, before and after school.

She seethed. She resented her life.

"I cannot wait to leave as soon as I turn eighteen," she admitted. "I hope to get a good husband." Nothing like this despicable man who was her father. At this point, Cindy absolutely hated him with every fiber of her being.

Girlie awoke from her tranquillized slumber, grateful that her daughter stepped up to prepare dinner, as, at this point, was incapable of doing anything strenuous. This was probably the most vicious beating she had ever received from her husband thus far!

Girlie hugged and thanked Cindy, praising her for her efforts. Cindy blushed as this was very unbecoming of her mother.

Probably the medication talking, she mused sarcastically.

Cindy assisted her mother in eating, as it was mandatory for her to eat before taking her medication every six hours.

It was almost seven o'clock, before Albert made an appearance, reeking of his favorite spirits, and the lingering scent of a woman's cheap perfume. He was totally drunk, to the point of falling over.

"Girlie!" He yelled.

"Where are you b****"!

Albert was furious.

Why was she not answering? He looked around and saw her on the couch, apparently asleep.

"Girlie!" He barked loudly. "Get the hell up. How can you be asleep, without giving me my food? Is this the thanks I get for working hard all day, whilst your lazy a** sleep all day?" he yelled.

Cindy appeared from her bedroom. "Hi Papa, Mammy, is not feeling well. She is on very strong pain medication that is making her sleepy," Cindy continued explaining, but her father interrupted.

"Did I ask you anything"? He grated through gritted teeth.

"No, Papa, but I just wanted to explain why Mammy is asleep now". Cindy firmly replied.

He charged toward his teenage daughter, who showed him no sign of fear.

He attempted to slap her but was so inebriated that he fell as soon as he flung his fist at her.

D***, rude slut! You are a w****just like that devil on the couch! I hate women!" he screamed at his daughter.

"None are no good!" "D*** nuisances, the whole lot of you! Roland and Jonah get your a**es in here and help me up," he demanded.

Both of them rushed over to do as they were commanded, overcome by fear. Cindy looked coldly at her father with pure, unadulterated hate.

As Albert sat on the armchair, he threw the water that Jonah brought, at his request, on his wife, startling her out of her medicated stupor. He laughed sinisterly.

"You are afraid of a little cold water, are you?"

Mocking her as the memory of why Jonah was born sickly, stood between them. That ominous night when she had to run and hide in the bushes from this monster that fathered her three children.

Girlie remained silent.

She gave him his supper, and began tidying up the kitchen. She was still very much impaired by the pain medication.

He ate, like a glutton, lapping up every last morsel of food. He came up to her and planted a hard, hateful kiss on her bruised lips, and a vicious slap on her derriere.

"You are nothing without me. Remember that, okay, b****!" he smirked menacingly.

He shoved her aside. She grimaced as her battered body could not handle any more pain at this point. He went to lay down.

Girlie finished tidying up and sat down. Her thoughts were whirling out of control. She took another dose of pain medication, much earlier than prescribed, unable to bear the throbbing that pulsed over her inflamed body.

By ten o'clock, she was delirious. She began hallucinating as she imagined that her husband was charging at her to "finish what he started," making good on his earlier threat.

She screamed. Jonah jumped up from sleeping.

"God, please don't let Mama be beaten again", he pleaded. "I can't wait to grow up! I will personally give Papa a good 'cut tail', for mercilessly beating on my mother!" he promised himself.

Jonah cautiously peered outside from his room, that he and Roland shared. The house was eerily quiet, but he distinctly remembered hearing his mother's screams earlier. Doubt gnawed at his mind; could it have been a dream? With careful, silent steps, he made his way to the bedroom of his parents. The unmistakable scent of kerosene hung heavily in the air. It was a smell he associated with burning garbage in the backyard, not inside the house.

Suddenly, flames erupted on his parents' bed, and the blood-curdling screams of his father pierced the silent night. Frozen in shock, Jonah watched in horror as his mother set his father on fire. Albert, engulfed in flames, thrashed about in agony, cursing at his wife amidst the inferno.

Girlie, realizing Jonah had witnessed her gruesome act, stared at him in horror.

She reached for him, knowing Cindy and Roland were also awakened by the nightmarish screams of their father.

"Run!" she hollered at her children, urgency lacing her voice. Without hesitation, they fled into the night as Albert's anguished cries echoed behind them.

Jonah was utterly horrified.

Completely stunned.

Overwhelmed with shock.

His mother killed his dad!!

CHAPTER NINE
FIERY TRIALS

1 Peter 4:12

Beloved, do not be surprised that a trial by fire is occurring among you, as if something strange is happening to you

Albert was hospitalized in ICU with third-degree burns. Girlie was taken into custody, pending investigations. The children were separated and placed in the care of guardians. Cindy went to one home, and Roland to another. The house was only partially burnt as the quick response of their neighbors came to his rescue, feverishly extinguishing the raging, angry blaze and speeding him to the hospital.

The whole village was ablaze with curious reporters and media personnel. The news of the "Albert & Girlie" tragedy became the talk of the entire twin island. Everyone flocked to Mayaro to receive any bit of information. The 'Curious', the 'Cynical' and the 'Concerned'.

The masses were salivating to find out more about this tiny woman, who was dubbed "the woman who set her husband on fire." This was the mid 1970's and this was newsworthy.

As the neighbors continued their speculations of what they perceived to have happened that eventful night, they wondered about the sole witness; ten-year-old Jonah who was now shielded at an undisclosed location.

Jonah had not said a word since that tragic night. Too shocked to utter even one syllable, his voice locked up as his brain grappled with the memories of that fiery night... his father, whom he loved in spite of it all, screaming in sheer agony! The howling pitch of his father's voice deeply embedded in his mind.

Albert truly suffered while he fought for whatever life was left in him. He received eighty-five percent burns about his body. After three horrendous weeks, Albert succumbed to his injuries, exacerbated by his contraction of pneumonia. News of his passing rocked the entire village, even though they knew it was inevitable, due to the severity of his burns, some were still hoping against hope, praying for his recovery - mainly his sisters.

Very few were casting blame upon Girlie. They were very well aware of the tragedies that Albert placed upon her and their children. Everyone knew what had transpired, especially the atrocities of the last two years in the Foster's household.

It was not a happy tale!

Tongues wagged in judgment as they spuriously disregarded her faith.

"Apparently, all her prayers were in vain."

"She couldn't pray the devil out of her husband," and "She sent her husband to a literal fiery 'hell'." Were just a few of their sarcastic summations.

Girlie was charged with first degree murder.

The outcry at this unfair charge slapped on this pitiful woman, grappled the entire village, as by now everyone had become aware of the distress and agony Girlie faced on a daily basis, that created a chaotic and toxic environment, not only to her, but her children!!!

As those assigned to the case investigated, many came forward with testimonies that Girlie, severely beaten on that very day, was heavily medicated and truly felt that she was in immediate danger. They recounted the times she had reached out to relevant authorities to help her, which were all ignored, and that the lack of assistance kept her children and herself in harm's way.

In addition, the villagers were shocked with the revelation that Albert had another family in another town. He had four other sons and one daughter from a common-law relationship with another woman, who he apparently had beaten to death. He had totally disregarded that part of his life and lived as if they did not exist.

This man, a force to be reckoned with, was both loved and hated, feared and adored. So ruggedly handsome with his sharp, chiseled jawline, fair complexion, and the most glorious head of hair, ever seen on a man apart from probably, Sampson of the Bible.

This enigma of a man, who lived as a daredevil, with no fear for God nor man. His life now snuffed out by a waif of a woman, at the age of forty-eight.

This renegade of a man, who believed that he was indestructible and invincible, diminished to just a pitiful memory to all who knew, loved and loathed him.

He ignored God, choosing disobedience. He lived a reckless life of wickedness, that came down upon his own head in this lifetime.

So heartbreakingly sad. The whole village and country were plunged into mourning, for the untimely death of Albert Foster.

Ecclesiastes 7:17 (NIV)

Do not be over wicked, and do not be a fool- why die before your time?

Hopefully his children's teeth would not be on edge for his partaking of sour grapes, (Ezekiel

18:2) was the woeful prediction on some of the villagers' lips.

Albert Foster was buried in an unmarked grave; with very few people gathering at his interment. All 8 of his children attended; too numb and shocked to shed any tears.

Cindy looked on at his final resting place, a smirk on her face.

Psalm 37:9/22 (KJV)

For evildoers shall be cut off: but those that wait upon the LORD, they shall inherit the earth

For such as be blessed of him shall inherit the earth; and they that be cursed of him shall be cut off.

Proverbs 5: 22- 23 (ESV)

The iniquities of the wicked ensnare him, and he is held fast in the cords of his sin. He dies for lack of discipline, and because of his great folly he is led astray.

CHAPTER TEN
JUSTICE LIKE WATER

AMOS 5:24

'But let justice roll down like waters, and righteousness like an ever-flowing stream'

'Hypocrisy at its finest,' was the only phrase that aptly described the feigned heartbreak of Albert's sisters, as they clamored for justice for their dead brother, but yet while he was alive, never called him out on his bad behavior. This became a civil war within the small, sleepy, previously unknown fishing village of Mafeking.

As Girlie stood trial, many came out in support of her. She was a badly battered and bruised housewife whose only fault was her unwavering loyalty to a beast that cared for nothing and no one and lived only to please himself. As the weeks rolled past, Girlie became increasingly depressed and suicidal as the reality of it all hit her.

She was a murderer!

Her children, separated from one another, were not even allowed to visit her as the authorities erroneously believed that she was unfit to see and be around her children.

Girlie believed that her children hated her for what she had done to their father. Her heart broke yet again upon recalling Jonah's horrified expression that fateful night. She literally was washed away with worry, as she knew how fragile her son was. She longed to speak to them and assure them that all will be well.

It had to be.

Her faith being all she had, Girlie fasted and prayed for complete deliverance and vindication.

Thoughts of "what if's" plagued her mind.

What if she is sentenced to jail for the remainder of her life?

What if she never sees her children again, especially Jonah?

What if her children grow up and bad things happen to them because of her many mistakes?

What if...

"Oh God, please help me!" was her tormented cry.

After a couple of grueling months, the trial ended with the closing remarks of her lawyer's appeal to reduce the sentence from murder to manslaughter.

The attorney cited the case **of R v Duffy 1949,** where a woman killed her sleeping husband with an ax after she was prevented from leaving the house with her child to escape years of alleged abuse. He continued his arguments based on the provocation of her actions - sadistic harm done to her with years of relentless beatings along with the verbal abuse she endured as Albert constantly threatened and belittled her with disparaging names.

"... the provocation must cause a ***sudden and temporary*** loss of self-control, rendering the accused so subject to passion as to make him/her for the moment not master of his mind."

Girlie Foster was convicted of manslaughter; sentenced to five years of imprisonment with possibility of a reduction of jail time based on good behavior and other factors. She would also have to apply to the courts, on her release for custody of Cindy, now 13, Jonah, 10 and Roland, 8 years of age. All children were now a ward of the state, to be placed in temporary foster care with guardians deemed fit by the court.

Girlie broke down, split between relief and despair.

How can any of this be fair?

She was abused and mistreated and in that temporary state of madness, did the unbelievable, as she was still in shock as to the gravity of her actions. She cried out to God to look after her children; she could not possibly survive not taking care of them.

Her children were her lifeline, especially Jonah, whose horrified face was indelibly imprinted in her mind.

How can she ever forgive herself for this?

At last, Girlie was able to see and hug her children; at the court room before being taken to her new home for the next five years. It was a bittersweet moment for all.

Jonah held on to his mom for dear life, the four months apart, seemed like an eternity to his grieving heart; pleading with the authorities to not take his mommy away. Having regained his voice a few weeks ago after going through some therapeutic sessions for ***psychogenic aphonia***, with a counsellor appointed by the court, Jonah's recorded testimony also aided in her charges being reduced from murder to manslaughter.

There was not a dry eye in the tiny courthouse as they were whisked off for the next few years to be raised by strangers......Jonah and Roland to one family and Cindy to another. A family torn apart. The exact replica of Girlie's heart.

"Lord, please take care of my children's heart and soul," she pleaded to her Father. "Never allow bitterness to take hold of them, and may your peace be their constant companion at all times," she continued in prayer. "Take good care of them and be both mother and father to them," Girlie implored.

Girlie felt so hopeless but her faith in God gave her the assurance that she needed to rely in faith and hope that her children would be properly taken care of... that favor with God and man will be upon them. Even if they were now without their biological parents, she knew that their Heavenly Father would cover them and keep her precious children safe.

CHAPTER ELEVEN
LIKE COLD WATER

Proverbs 25:25

"Like cold water to a thirsty soul, so is good news from a far country"

Jonah awoke from another one of his nightmares. The sight of his burning father, a constant companion in his dreams. Two and a half years had passed since that fateful night where he and his siblings lost both their parents. Two years and two months since he last saw his mother. They were not allowed to visit her, relying only on family members and friends who visited her from time to time, carrying hugs, love and kisses.

Jonah was about to turn, when he realized that his side of the bed was soaked! Jonah had wet the bed!

Oh, my goodness!

He felt ashamed. Disgust covered him like a blanket. He had never done this before and had no understanding of how to process this.

Jonah and Roland were temporarily placed into the care of Miss Lorna, a very kind, humble lady. Together with her husband and two sons, they took on the responsibility of looking after them both, ensuring that they were not separated. This family did everything in their power to make a comfortable home for the two boys.

Now here it was, Jonah found himself repaying them with a wet bed! He began sobbing silently.

"Why are you crying?" The voice said. It was a voice that often spoke to him since the death of his father.

"Just roll Marlon over to your side, and go back to sleep," the voice compelled.

Jonah complied.

This is good.

"It will appear as if their son did it and not me so I will not be punished," he reasoned with a smile.

The next morning, Marlon's screams of anguish echoed throughout the village as he received a whooping for his misdemeanor. Marlon pleaded his innocence, while Jonah stood and looked on, relieved that he had listened to the voice that got him out of trouble.

Jonah began falling behind in school. Simple assignments became insurmountable as his brain became foggy and unable to comprehend anything. He started fighting in school, constantly on high alert, feeling the need to defend himself against perceived dangers.

Eventually, he became the school bully. Everyone, in awe of his presence, attempted their best to be on his good side. As an angry Jonah was likened to the Marvel character of "THE INCREDIBLE HULK," - the more enraged, the stronger he seemed.

It gave Jonah a sense of power.

Exhilaration.

A high that not even the marijuana he began smoking gave him! Bullying empowered him, as he vowed to be scared of no one and nothing. EVER!!

At almost 13 years, Jonah was a very handsome lad. He took after his father with his hair and light complexion, while his brother and sister took after their mother. He felt superior. Girls were already running after him, and the boys wanted to be his friend. He was very popular and relished the attention.

At home, he was the perfect son, always obedient and never one to get into trouble. Hence, his foster mother, Miss Lorna, refused to believe some of the tales she was told.

Not her Jonah!

They were lying about that poor child!

Hadn't he been through enough? All three of them!

In the third year of his mom's incarceration, rumors circulated that she might be released soon. Girlie prayed every night for her children, thanking God that they all seemed to be doing well despite what they have been through. They were literally torn apart, but somehow God sustained everyone in the midst of the mess. She offered up another heartfelt prayer to heaven.

Confirmation came that Girlie was indeed being released by the end of July of 1979. Originally supposed to be released at the end of 1980, she was granted an early release due to her good behavior and contrite, humble disposition.

Jonah, Roland and Cindy were finally reunited at the end of November of 1979 with their mother. Girlie applied for custody of her children, a mandate of the court. It was not automatic as they had to be certain she was mentally fit to take care of them.

There were tears of joy as they all hugged and kissed their mother after four years apart. Cindy had turned 17, Jonah was almost 14 and Roland had just celebrated his 12th birthday.

Girlie couldn't believe how much they had grown. Cindy had blossomed into quite a beautiful young lady. Jonah was going to be a heartbreaker, taking after his father in looks - she quietly prayed that was all that he took and Roland was taller than her!

Girlie and Jonah's birthdays, along with Christmas, were to be truly celebrated this year. They were very thankful that God had brought them through the worst and appreciated being restored as a family, albeit minus one. They expected true peace, as the bickering and fights would now be history.

They all looked forward to putting the fractured pieces of their lives back together under the banner of the Lord Jesus Christ.

CHAPTER TWELVE
PURE WATER

Hebrews 10:22

"...Let us draw near with a true heart in full assurance of faith, with our hearts sprinkled clean from an evil conscience and our bodies washed with pure water"

Girlie settled back into society with the help of God, making her home a place where worship and prayer were the focal points of their lives. After her initial shock at the extreme changes in her children, life became settled in the 'Foster' household.

Memories of her deceased husband still plagued her mind. His clothes, and personal belongings still were at the house; she refused to get rid of them. She missed him deeply. She still could not come to terms with the fact that her own hands brought about his untimely demise. Neither she nor the children spoke about it. Neighbors dared not broach the subject, so it was accepted that it was not to be spoken about... ever!

Much to her mother's surprise, Cindy had a boyfriend. They met at church and she was excited for her mother to meet him. His name was Kenny Graham – tall, dark and handsome with a love for music as he played the bass guitar at the church that she had attended with her adopted family. While Girlie was happy that he was a Christian boy, she felt that with all that had happened over the last few years, Girlie had somewhat lost connection with her daughter, who appeared to eagerly want to move into the next chapter of her life. Cindy was way too young, Girlie admitted, but with her own heart still tattered and torn, she felt that she was not "motherly" enough to raise the reservations she felt about the budding romance between her daughter and this man that Cindy was so enamored by.

Jonah, seemed reticent, and lost in his own world. She thought of obtaining some psychological help for him. Her pastor tried counseling him, but to no avail. Jonah, with a mind of his own, and sometimes a mind within a mind, revealed to her that he heard voices that compelled him to say and do certain things that led to behavior unbecoming to who she knew Jonah to be.

Roland appeared unbothered by everything, always happy and jolly. His temperament changed only when he and his brother were involved in a physical altercation. That was something new and it bothered her immensely. Everything was the same yet changed.

Girlie spent most of her days in prayer and Bible study. She had given her life to the Lord before she got married to Albert, but true consecration to her Savior, came to fruition during her time spent behind bars.

She sought and pleaded for forgiveness from the Lord, as she spent years in relentless remorse and deep regret. Days turned into nights as she wrestled with the weight of her actions, the guilt heavy upon her heart like an unyielding burden. Tears streamed down her face, mingling with the prayers that poured from her lips, each word a plea for redemption and peace.

Then, one day the room filled with a sense of Divine Presence, an overwhelming aura of Love and Grace that enveloped her like a gentle, cleansing stream. The very essence of the agape love of God washing over her, with pure water. All the stains of guilt and shame that clung to her soul - all gone; and in that sacred moment, surrounded by the redemptive embrace of her Savior, she felt a deep sense of release.

It was then and only then that she found the strength to truly forgive herself. The weight that had burdened her for so long lifted, replaced by a profound sense of peace and freedom. The tears that fell now were not of sorrow, but of gratitude and joy. She knew in her heart that she was forgiven, that God's love had washed away her past transgressions, leaving her soul cleansed and renewed.

She got a job at the County Council, the department in charge of the care of the road infrastructure in her village. She was grateful for such an opportunity, believing it came from God Himself. It also paid very well. Her aim now was to make a good life for her children. Her thoughts of them were the only things that kept her sane. She was truly thankful; thankful for her children, thankful for her second chance at life, and for her faith in God that never left her nor forsook her. Now her children were different people, and she had to rely solely on God to get through this as the trauma and pain they all had experienced had affected them in various ways.

Jonah was no longer interested in school, as his mind continually obstructed his learning capabilities. No matter how hard he tried, the knowledge from the books was not getting past that impenetrable blockage. Constantly in trouble, he bullied both boys and girls. He constantly ran away from school, breaking his arms on two separate occasions. The intensity of his fights with his brother was escalating to the point that he threw an iron at Roland, knocking him out cold!

Girlie prevailed in prayer. She knew that God was able to mend and repair everything that the enemy had disrupted in their lives.

He is the repairer of the breach!

ISAIAH 58:12 KJV

And they that shall be of thee shall build the old waste places; thou shalt raise up the foundation of many generations; and thou shalt be called, The Repairer of the breach; the restorer of paths to dwell in.

CHAPTER THIRTEEN
ROCK OF MY REFUGE

2 Samuel 22:2 -3

"The LORD is my Rock and my fortress, and my deliverer. The GOD of my rock; in Him will I trust: HE is my Shield, and the Horn of my salvation, my high tower and my refuge, my Savior; thou savest me from violence"

Jonah's fractured childhood led to instability and dependency issues that would plague him almost all his life. He was deprived of the continuous nurturing and affection from both his parents, bestowed upon because of his illness from birth.

This insouciant, wild child became a 'stray bullet,' a law unto himself. He reveled in boldly and shamelessly fearing no one and nothing. With his captivating looks, Jonah easily charmed his way out of any situation. He became a favorite among everyone, his charismatic aura allowing him to bend rules as he pleased.

Having abandoned his education, he gravitated towards a dubious group of young delinquents led by the notorious Steve Romeo. It was through this association that he was introduced to the dark world of guns. Together, they roamed the neighboring farms, brazenly pilfering livestock – from cattle and goats to sheep and chickens – all for the sake of turning a profit.

Jonah indulged recklessly, smoking marijuana, snorting cocaine, and consuming alcohol without restraint. He chased puncheon rum with CARIB beer, dubbing it 'brass and steel', carousing in the potent mixture. At the tender age of 15, he became sexually active, attracting girls like bees to honey. Jonah paid scant regard to their ages; life for him was an unending, intoxicating high from which he refused to descend.

Meanwhile, his mother battled for him in prayer. Jonah tried to shield this side of his life from her, knowing that she had suffered enough. But the active Spirit of God within her had her pleading on her knees for her son. She knew Jonah was meant for greater things, with an integral role to play in the Kingdom. His calling and election were sealed from his incubation in her womb. She continuously cried out to God for this fulfillment over his life.

Jonah didn't care; he sincerely felt justified in his actions. To him, life was a debt owed, and he made sure to collect – heedless of the casualties left in his wake. But that was the secret side of Jonah. On the outside, he was all charm and wit, effortlessly winning over everyone he encountered. His typical days were spent lounging on the street corners, chatting nonsense with his 'boys' and watching the offshore workers head to their job sites. Deep down, he harbored a hint of envy, yearning for a life different from the one he lived.

One fateful Saturday night, Jonah led his gang as the main gunman to a neighboring farm. Their target: cattle and sheep, valuable assets they intended to steal and sell for profit. With Christmas drawing near, they had eager buyers lined up readily waiting for their ill-gotten gains.

"Who's there?" they almost jumped out of their skin at the sudden command.

This was unexpected. They scouted the area and deemed it safe.

"Jonah!" Steve whispered frantically, "we better get out of here! This place is secured, and we can't be caught! Let's go!"

Jonah snickered. "NO!"

"We're not leaving without the prize. We need money for the season, and this new 'chick' of mine has her eyes on these earrings. I'm going to get them for her. She makes it worthwhile, if you know what I mean," Jonah insinuated.

"I said who is out there!" screamed the unknown voice. "I have a bloody gun and am not afraid to use it! You pesky nuisance only running around stealing people's livestock. I WILL SHOOT AND KILL YOUR DUMB A****! You scum of the earth! I will make a d*** example of you tonight!"

Jonah cocked his gun, "I will make an example of you tonight," he snarled with emphasis.

He pulled the trigger three times but the gun refused to fire!

What happened?

Upon examination, the cartridge appeared disfigured and dented, refusing to explode.

What sheer madness! That's impossible!!

Steve grabbed Jonah's arms, "Let's get out of here, NOW! THIS is getting out of hand! You almost killed a man. We may be thieves, but murder is where I draw the line, Jonah. Let's GO!"

Jonah was puzzled. How did that gun not fire? Was it his mother's prayers protecting him? They ran as fast as they could while Steve scolded Jonah for what he almost did.

What had come over him tonight?

Jonah came to a stark realization – he had harbored murderous intentions toward an innocent man. In that moment, he came face to face with himself, and what he saw within was unsettling. Jonah did not like the darkness that lurked inside him.

CHAPTER FOURTEEN
WAVER BETWEEN TWO

1 KINGS 18:21

"How long will you waver between two opinions? If the LORD is GOD, follow HIM; but if Baal is god, follow him"

Jonah was restless, as thoughts of what almost occurred, tormented him throughout the night.

After stashing the illegal firearms away at their customary hideout combined with their other "goodies" for sale – (a euphemism for their illegal narcotics)- they parted ways to their respective homes.

Jonah was awakened by a loud banging at the door.

What the hell?

His mother and siblings scrambled to see what the commotion was about. It was three am in the morning!

"Ma'am, is your son, Jonah, at home?" was the brisque question addressed to Girlie.

"Yes, he is and has been all night," Girlie lied to the four burly police officers. Begging for forgiveness at the same time underneath her breath.

"Are you sure?" they queried. "We have a description that matches your son that puts him at the scene of an attempted robbery at the farm two miles away."

"Attempted? Nothing was taken and you come here in the middle of the night with a fake robbery that you are tagging my son in? As I said, all my children were at home with me tonight and that's my final answer!"

With the door closing behind her, Cindy, visibly upset, turned to Jonah in anger. "Look at what you've done. Your behavior is pushing mother into sin. She lied to the police because of you!"

"Cindy", her mother's tone was stern.

"What??? Can't you see what Jonah is. A bad seed. Corrupted. A 16-year-old school dropout! He is no good, and not a good example for Roland either! You may be blind, but I am not, and he is just like Papa! We have Papa here again!"

Jonah was just about to retaliate but Girlie interrupted him.

"I will not have you speaking about Jonah like that. He may be confused, but he is a good boy. He is a man of God and a man after God's plan and heart."

Cindy laughed scornfully, "Really? Mama, you have always favored Jonah and saw me as nobody and nothing. I am the good child. Always obedient and doing all that is right! But did you ever see that? No! Because it's Jonah this and Jonah that. He just cannot do any wrong for you. Always shielding and protecting him! That's why I don't like you, Jonah," she turned to address him face to face. "You are selfish, arrogant, prideful and mean." "You may have Mama fooled and most of the people in this village, but I know who you are, and no number of prayers can ever save you," she screeched in tears.

"He is nothing like my Kenny," she boasted. "Now, that is a true man of God! You should take some pages out of his book, Jonah!"

She cried as she ran into her bedroom, slamming the door. Jonah and Roland were stunned. They never saw that side of their sister. Girlie just shook her head. She figured that Cindy wanted an excuse to get away from them as the infatuation for Kenny had intensified and they were beginning to speak about marriage. She had a nice little clerical job at a regional corporation in the area and seemed to have her life put together. She attended church regularly with her boyfriend, and was very obedient as she indicated.

Girlie shrugged. She tried so hard to be both mother and father for them, but she guessed Cindy was not doing well, after all. She seldom complained about anything, but apparently had a lot of resentment towards Jonah.

"Jonah and Roland, go back to bed. But Jonah, you and I need to have a talk tomorrow and I am taking you to church to see Pastor Khan, okay? No arguments!"

After church, Girlie pulled Jonah into a meeting with Pastor Khan. She explained to the pastor and his wife what she was enduring. She knew that Jonah loved the Lord at one time but had gotten involved with the wrong company and needed spiritual guidance. Pastor Khan and his wife assured Girlie that they would speak with him.

Jonah knew what they were going to say and frankly, he was not interested. He was having fun and he loved this life. Easy money, pretty girls, partying, drinking... why must he give up all that for church? The music was dull, the girls plain and uninteresting, not putting out anything and the sermons equally as boring.

HOW LONG DO YOU INTEND TO RUN, JONAH?

A voice boomed from nowhere in his ear!

Jonah nearly flipped over in the pew.

What or who was that?

He looked around. His mom and the pastor were engrossed in conversation, and there was no one else around.

"Wow! Another voice in my head now?" He mused.

He already had one voice constantly speaking to him, and now this one?

"I am probably going crazy," he concluded, half-jokingly.

Jonah agreed to meet with the pastor later in the evening. Jonah felt he was at a crossroads with confusion. He did sometimes feel a tug at his heart when he was out partying and having sexual relations with all those pretty girls.

And now, that VOICE!

Something about that voice.

Jonah met with the Pastor. After an intense conversation, the man of God began prophesying over his life, endorsing the call that his mother constantly spoke over him almost daily!!

After agreeing to come to church more often, he left. Jonah knew full well he had no intention of making good on his promise to attend church regularly. He laughed.

They are so gullible.... the whole lot of them!

COME TO ME ALL WHO ARE HEAVY LADEN!

That VOICE again!

Next Sunday, Jonah feigned sickness, promising to be in church next time. Instead, he decided to go for a swim in the Ortoire River. The day was oppressively humid, and the persistent voice inside his head urged him to go.

Jonah wasn't a strong swimmer, but he figured that there would be others around. Strangely, he found himself alone. It seemed like everyone else wanted to be "good" and attend church today. He chuckled to himself.

The place was inviting and serene; the susurrus of the leaves whispered in the gentle breeze, creating a peaceful ambiance. Jonah submerged himself into the cool, inviting, crystalline water, a welcome relief against his burning skin. The scorching sun mingled with the coolness, bringing refreshment to his dried soul. He swam up and down the river, feeling the ebb and flow of its gentle waves caressing his body like a soothing lover. The weightlessness of the water gave him a sense of freedom, a release from the rules of gravity. Jonah felt he could swim there forever, in this tranquil underwater world. Jonah momentarily forgot who or where he was.

Oh God!

Suddenly, a sharp cramp seized his legs, followed by a heaviness in his arms. Fatigued gripped him, his entire body shutting down in weariness.

"HELP!" he cried out in pain. "Someone, anybody, please help me," his voice barely audible.

Glancing around in fear and desperation, he spotted a rope tied to one of the trees. It was too far, and he didn't have the strength to reach it.

Will this be my last swim ever?

Is this it?

Am I going to drown?

To die?

The chaotic thoughts swirled around his head.

"No, Jonah," the demonic voice lied. "Allow yourself to sink, and you can walk out, once you have reached the bottom!"

Relief flooded him at the suggestion, and he inhaled deeply, allowing himself to be totally immersed.

That deceptive voice wanted Jonah dead.

CHAPTER FIFTEEN
HE RESTORES MY SOUL

PSALMS 23:3(a) (NKJV)

"He restores my soul"

Deo Kalicharan and Krishna Dhunda, Vishnu's brother, set off for the next village hoping to catch a ride. They had been called for a private job and were eager to earn some extra cash for the upcoming holidays, as money was very tight.

As they approached the Ortoire River, a faint cry caught their attention. They exchanged glances before Krishna exclaimed, "Did you hear that? Sounds like someone's at the river!' Without hesitation, they ran toward the sound, a weak cry for help.

Arriving just in time, they saw someone being submerged in the water. The river was clean and clear, making it easier to spot the body.

Deo went in first, instructing Krishna to heave the victim from underneath. They both knew that a panicked victim could endanger all of them, so they carefully lifted Jonah, whose almost lifeless body weighed a ton, struggling to bring him to safety.

Once on the bank, they tilted Jonah's head and lifted his chin to open his airways. He was barely breathing and semi-conscious. They placed him in a supine position with his head turned sideways allowing the ingested water to expel.

Recognizing him, they exclaimed, "It's Jonah!"

"Hey, what were you doing out here alone? It's never a good idea to come out here by yourself. You see what almost happened to you!? How do you think your mother would take this news? You want to kill Miss Girlie, or something? Thank God we were here to rescue you; otherwise, she might be preparing for a funeral this Christmas!"

They continued scolding him, talking about the 'what if's" and declaring themselves his godfathers from now on.

"God orchestrated this rescue mission for you, man," Deo continued.

"Maybe it's time to start going to church," Krishna advised.

Jonah felt deeply ashamed; he was supposed to be in church that day, but had disobeyed and came to the river instead. They assisted him to the health facility, where he was quickly attended to.

Jonah headed home, thankfully, his mother and siblings hadn't returned from church just yet. Exhausted, and filled with mixed emotions, Jonah went straight to bed and slept most of the day.

As he lay there, Jonah reflected on his life. He had nearly died, and where would he have gone? Eternally speaking?

He was supposed to be in the house of the Lord that day, but instead he did his own thing, leaning on the arm of flesh, and his own understanding.

Maybe Cindy was right about him - a spoiled, entitled bastard expecting the world to revolve around him because of the many mishaps in his life. He didn't want to be part of this world anymore. Tormented day and night, struggling to sleep, filled with anxiety every day.

He felt useless.

"No job, no money, just living on the edge," he thought. His encounters with women only left him feeling used; his youth and virility had been their attraction. But now, faced with his mortality, he made a decision.

Eternity was just one breath away... or rather minus one breath away.

Lord, I will follow you.

I hear you.

You brought me back from the brink of death, and I am so thankful.

For Girlie, this was the best Christmas. All her children attended church and decided to follow the Lord's ways, forsaking the world with all its evil and wickedness.

The New Year of 1982, brought an unexpected blessing – Jonah was offered an incredible job at the prestigious oil company, AMOCO, a position for which he was in no way qualified. They employed him as a floorman at their Galeota headquarters in Guayaguayare.

Girlie was taken aback at the goodness and favor from God' because this exceeded her expectations. She never could have dreamt or imagined that he was going to be employed with the 'big guns.'

She wanted him gainfully employed but this was more than she had asked or imagined.

She cried and cried in exuberance, praising and thanking God not only for this job, but for saving her son from self-destruction. Girlie wept and wailed in intercession for her son, and now she was visibly reaping the rewards of answered prayer and supplication!

Jonah was ecstatic; he finally felt useful, and the maddening rage that consumed him before was completely obliterated, from his mind, will and emotions. He experienced the peace of a restored soul.

Finally!

CHAPTER SIXTEEN
Be zealous and Repent

Revelations 3:19 (ESV)

'To those whom I love, I reprove and discipline, so be zealous and repent.

Jonah became zealous for the LORD, reading the Bible, day and night with a fervor that bordered on obsession. His work rotation of fourteen days at home and fourteen days offshore allowed him the time to dive into the Scriptures upon his return. This extreme behavior troubled his mother, who couldn't quite grasp the intensity of his religious zeal, speaking things that she failed to understand. To others, Jonah seemed to breathe out the Scriptures as easily as air and devoured them like food.

By this time, Cindy was thoroughly fed up with her brother's antics, and mockingly called him a "crazy bat." She decided to escape it all by marrying her beloved and leave "the mad house" in reference to the family home.

Various pastors visited Jonah, hoping to understand and getting to the bottom of his bizarre behavior. They cleansed the home of possible demonic artifacts that may be the cause, but ultimately, left more puzzled than enlightened. They all agreed on one thing: Jonah was special with a significant calling on his life.

One pastor even suggested the unthinkable - that Jonah should stop reading the bible altogether.

In truth, Jonah was experiencing "Theia mania" or divine madness, often associated with unconventional, outrageous, unexpected or unpredictable behavior linked to religious or spiritual pursuit. To mainstream society, these patterns of behavior may seem to be symptoms of mental illness, but are actually a manifestation of enlightenment by people who had transcended societal norms.

Jonah longed to discover his place and purpose in God's will. He felt a deep spiritual connection, akin to the spirit of John the Baptist. Unfortunately, the lack of spiritual discernment in those around him led to misunderstanding and mislabels.

Despite this, Jonah excelled at his job and was soon promoted to power tong operator. The favor of God was unmistakable upon him; the company bosses appreciated his work ethic and diligence. Jonah's career soared, with hints of a possible job offer in the U.S.A. on the horizon. This news thrilled Jonah, and he couldn't help but exclaim, 'Lord, you are so good to me!"

One weekend during his off time, Jonah and three friends from church decided to take a sabbatical and ventured to Cedar Grove Hill. They camped out in prayer and intercession for God's favor and grace. After a powerful session experiencing the Glory of the Lord, they fell into a deep sleep, exhausted.

In the wee hours of the morning, Jonah was awoken by a Presence in the tent. It beckoned him out into the open, where he fell on his knees. A blinding, pure Light surrounded them all, rendering him speechless in Its Presence. By now, the other three friends were awakened, and they too fell to their knee in awe and surrender.

Something shifted within Jonah. He felt a spirit "jump" inside him, a sensation he couldn't quite explain. When they packed up and left, each man was left puzzled, unsure if it was a shared dream or a divine encounter. It felt so surreal and celestial and none were certain of its implications. The men were all puzzled and disoriented as what they had all experienced was phenomenal. They were afraid to say anything to anyone since Jonah was already being labeled as "crazy" and they were afraid to be tarred with that same brush.

Jonah began to join his mother at her weekly prayer sessions at home, exuding a magnetic presence that intrigued the women in the group. He would pray for and with them, one woman even remarked that she felt "heavenly" and did not want to leave that euphoric place.

Walking in the light and glory of his Father, Jonah felt a zeal and love that he had never known before. He longed to stay in this place of divine presence.

A grand crusade was planned to come to the village, organized by a foreign group and a neighboring pastor. Jonah eagerly anticipated attending, hungering for more and more of God's glory. The three nights of the crusade were powerful beyond measure. By the final night, Jonah felt as though he stood at Heaven's doors, never wanting to return to the mundane ways of earthly life. Overwhelmed, he cried out and surrendered his life to God once again, asking the Holy Spirit to take complete control.

Then, it happened.

His head began to spin, and delirium overtook him as the Spirit of God manifested in an overwhelming presence.

People watched on in horror, unsure of what they were witnessing!

Was it demons?

Was Jonah losing his mind?

Girlie, beside herself with worry, began to pray fervently for her son. "Lord, help him!" she pleaded.

Jonah couldn't bear it any longer. With fire seemingly all around him and an Awesome Presence too much to endure, he ran out of the assembly, collapsing under the weight of what can he can only describe as a divine encounter.

CHAPTER SEVENTEEN
HE THAT DWELLS

PSALM 91 (NKJV)

He that dwell in the secret place of the Most High shall abide under the shadow of the Almighty

Jonah lay unconscious, his body limp and barely breathing, as a crowd of curious onlookers gathered around him. Among them his frantic mother, pushing her way through the throng, crying out for someone to fetch a doctor.

Frantically, they rushed him to the nearest health facility where Dr. Ferdinand attended urgently to him. Baffled by his sudden collapse, the medical team ran a battery of tests to determine the cause. As Jonah slowly regained consciousness, a bright light shining in his eyes startled him back to awareness. Disoriented and confused, he found himself hooked up to machines and IV drips, with his mother and brother-in-law, Kenny, by his side.

"What happened?" he asked, his voice betraying his bewilderment.

"Oh, Jonah, you gave us such a fright,' Girlie, his mother, exclaimed with a mix of relief and worry. "You were acting so erratically, then suddenly passed out in front of the tent. We rushed you to see Dr. Ferdinand, and now after more than eight hours unconscious, you've finally woken up. We have no idea what's going on with you.... ever since you went up to Cedar Grove Hill, you've been so different.... it's like some kind of madness has taken hold of you...." she rambled.

Jonah didn't allow her to finish her rant, scoffing at the notion, insisting he was fine and attributing it to exhaustion. However, Kenny, deeply concerned and ignoring Jonah's dismissive attitude, turned to Dr. Ferdinand for an explanation. The doctor, equally puzzled, recommended immediate admission to the main hospital in the south, for a thorough diagnosis and proper treatment.

Without hesitation, Girlie and Kenny arranged for Jonah to be transported to the recommended hospital and admitted to Ward 10 – unbeknownst to Jonah, the ward designated for mental health patients.

There, after a series of assessments by psychiatrists, Jonah was diagnosed with manic depression/bipolar disorder. He was prescribed medication to manage his symptoms, but unfortunately, it seemed to exacerbate his condition. What were once subtle voices in his head now became a cacophony of screaming hallucinations, tormenting him relentlessly, day and night.

After a month of hospitalization, Jonah was discharged with a sobering warning to his mother that he might require lifelong medication, and continued care at the local health center. Overwhelmed with grief, Girlie refused to accept such a grim diagnosis for her beloved son. She was convinced that Jonah was called by God to do incredible things and be a beacon of light to many.

"He dwells in the secret place of God, and abides there!" She declared with her faith set as flint.

There's no way on God's green earth will she allow her beloved son to live life any other way. She resolutely decided that Satan can never destroy what God had ordained before Jonah's conception!

Kenny, however, recognized the gravity of the situation. He believed that Jonah's condition needed careful management; that the doctor's advice should not be taken lightly. Turning to Girlie, he offered his support, "I know Cindy was only too eager to move out, but I think that you need help with Jonah, as I can see the toll it's taking on you. With your permission, we will move back in to help you with Jonah," he offered graciously.

Girlie heaved a sigh of relief!!

Thank God I do not have to do this alone.

Jonah needed a father figure, and grateful that her son -in -law stepped up to offer the assistance that she desperately needed in this battle for her son's well-being!

Together, they would face this challenge head-on, determined to see Jonah through this difficult time.

CHAPTER EIGHTEEN
DO NOT WRESTLE AGAINST FLESH AND BLOOD

Ephesians 6:12 ESV

"For we do not wrestle against flesh and blood, but against the rulers, against the authorities, against the cosmic powers over this present darkness, against the spiritual forces of evil in the heavenly places"

And what a wrestle it became. Jonah's condition grew more maniacal with each passing day. Cindy was reluctant about moving back to her childhood home, especially for Jonah's sake, but her husband had convinced her that it was the Christian thing to do and her mother needed the support.

God's Hand of Favor seemed to remain upon Jonah, as his boss accepted the temporary leave of absence, promising that he could rejoin the company whenever he was able. What amazing grace abounded for Jonah.

However, despite the prayers and hopes, his episodes of madness became more psychotic, and the prescribed medication offered no relief.

In one harrowing episode Jonah nearly killed himself during a manic episode that led him to the neighbor's sliding front door. He broke through the glass, miraculously escaping without injury. Girlie intensified her prayers for her son, pleading with the Lord for his deliverance from this madness.

On another terrifying night, as Girlie attempted to give Jonah his medication, he almost bit off her finger and pushed her so hard she fell against a large hutch in the living room, resulting in what appeared to be a cracked rib!!

Kenny took immediate action.

With the help of Roland and the neighbors, they violently subdued Jonah, restraining him until the ambulance arrived to take him to St. Ann's Psychiatric Hospital. Seeing the severity of Jonah's condition, Kenny also advised Cindy to escort Girlie to the local emergency room, as she was in extreme pain from her injuries and emotional distress at seeing her son in such a state.

The entire scenario was chaotic and filled with anguish. Kenny scolded Girlie, "Mama, you need to face the reality that Jonah is out of his mind, out of control and is not safe for you or anyone to be around; just look at him" .... Jonah was yelling and hurling obscenities and insults through his bruised and bloodied lips, his eyes menacingly black in psychotic rage, grunting like a wild animal as he unsuccessfully tried to escape from the restraining ropes around his ankles and hands.

"Cindy, sweetheart, take your mother to the emergency room. She needs urgent attention!" Kenny's stern command echoed through the chaos.

Hours later, the paramedics arrived, finding Jonah somewhat calmer from exhaustion. He was quickly loaded into the ambulance to be transported to the hospital, where he was admitted to the ward reserved for serious mental cases.

There existed an old wives' tale that once you spent time in there, you were a permanent lunatic with little to no hope of ever being in your "right mind" ever again! It was an absolute stigma to even be admitted in there; people will refer to you as having "mad papers". It was a hopeless situation and one that Girlie had been praying against from the inception of this traumatic turn of events.

Two months had passed before Girlie was finally able to venture out to finally visit her son, taking time to heal from the wounds and bruises inflicted unknowingly by Jonah on that eventful night that sealed his fate. With each step her heart grew heavier as she wasn't sure what state her precious son would be in...Kenny having gone a couple times to visit Jonah, did not elaborate much as to what was really going on with Jonah...

As she entering the ward where they had her son confined, her heart shattered into a million pieces. What she saw before her was not her son, but an emaciated, disheveled, unkempt, badly beaten and naked man. Jonah was hog-tied to his bed, muttering to himself incoherently!! His once strong body now bore the scars of his ordeal, with needle markings covering his buttocks and upper arms.

"My God, My God", she cried out in anguish.

What sin did I commit that my son has to drink this bitter gall!!

Was he paying for Albert's sins?

My sins?

Is this the condition that my son will be for his entire life?

A shell of a human; never to experience the joys of wife, or children?

Tears streamed down her face as she poured out her heart to her Father in heaven. Sitting on a chair beside Jonah's bed, she called his name softly.

"Jonah?" she moaned.

At the sound of his name, Jonah's weary, bloodshot eyes lit up, and he burst into tears. In a hoarse, raspy voice, he began to recount the horrific events he had endured since being admitted to the mental institution. Girlie's heart clenched with pain as she listened to his tales of abuse, beatings and being stripped naked by the other patients, bullying him, confiscating all his clothes.

A burning sensation engulfed her abdomen, akin to her horrific experience that night where she sought solace in the terror of night, fleeing from her husband's abusive behavior, with three-year-old Cindy......

Girlie shuddered at the conjured image.

She hurriedly untied his shackles, and helped him dress. She had prepared his favorite meal and spoon-fed it to him, a sense of déjà vu coming over her, as she went back in time where she did this very same thing for a very frail and sickly Jonah many years ago.

Inwardly, she recoiled with anguish, When would this fight with flesh and blood end?

When will these demonic strongholds in her son's life be totally demolished once and for all?

When will reprieve for my son finally come?

As she hugged her beloved son, she made him a promise. Life would somehow get better. The stigma of being in the "mad house" would not define him. He would rise above it all and become the man of God she knew he was destined to be.

CHAPTER NINETEEN
HIS UNFAILING LOVE

Psalm 36:5-7

Your unfailing love, O Lord, is as vast as the heavens, your faithfulness is like the mighty mountains; your justice like the ocean's depth

Girlie sat across from the Chief Psychiatrist, Dr. Dianne Percell, her heart heavy with concern for her son Jonah. The doctor explained that Jonah's repeated attempts to escape had landed him among the "hardened" patients, where he had suffered merciless beatings at their hands.

Desperate to have him removed to a safer place, as she feared for his life, Girlie pleaded with the doctors. But they informed her that as long as Jonah continued to resist the authority of the institution, they had no choice but to keep him in the high-security ward.

"Mrs. Foster", Dr. Percell continued, "your son has been telling us that the voices in his head are urging him to run away. He sees us as the enemy, trying to harm him, and he refuses to take the "poison" we're offering. Our staff is aware that he attempted to bite off your fingers, when you tried giving him his medicine, which led you to admitting him to this hospital in the first place, so, we had no choice but to administer the medication intravenously."

That will explain those needle scars!!

Girlie's heart sank at the thought of the needle scars she had seen on Jonah's body earlier. How much medication were they pumping into him for his body to be grossly scarred like that?

Unable to bear the thought of her son suffering in such a place, Girlie embarked on a three-day Esther fast, praying fervently for the complete deliverance of her son; this was not the destiny God had shown her for her son.

She knew that surviving multiple near-death-experiences, had been a miracle, but now Jonah was in what Trini's called "the mad house." Death might have seemed a kinder fate, for few returned from such places with their sanity intact. The drugs alone had severe side effects, not to mention the hostile and volatile environment.

She didn't want this.... but her son-in-law Kenny had insisted. She could not be angry with him; he was only looking out for her and Jonah's well-being.

Kenny and Cindy had moved out once more, opting to live nearby to his own mother, Mrs. Phyllis Graham; she lived alone as all of her other children had migrated to the U.S.A. and England.

Roland, began a serious relationship with Candy Francois, a very pretty and vivacious young girl from the area. They seemed to be very much in love and he was seldom at home, most days and nights were spent at her residence. Girlie disapproved of his lifestyle, but as he reminded his mother, he was over 18 years and therefore an adult. Unfortunately, he was already drinking and smoking just like his father; but Candy seemed to love him as is, so what could she do?

Right now, Jonah was her priority. If he could show the doctors that he was calm, compliant, and taking his medication, they just might send him home under her care once more. So, she prayed and fasted, knowing the power of her petitions to God.

Meanwhile, Jonah, was determined to escape from the hospital. How in the world he got there, was a mystery to him, but he was fully aware of what they wanted to do!! Those people in white were cloaked in darkness, out to kill him, and he needed to get out! He was tired of the needles, the forced medicating and the constant surveillance.

He made a deceitful oath to the doctors that he would take the medication orally.

However, the Voice inside his head had told him to hide the medication beneath his upper lip and gum, tricking the nurses during their checks. It was his only way out.

As time passed, with Girlie's continuous unwavering support, prayers and visits, Jonah's mind miraculously began to stabilize. It was a mystery to the doctors, who had witnessed a total transformation. Where he was once filled with rage and violent behavior, had now turned to extremely polite cooperation. Jonah helped made the beds, assisted the nurses, and showed kindness to the other patients.

Girlie never wavered in her faith and prayers. She knew that Lord would guide her and intervene for her son. Bargaining with heaven for Jonah's sound mind, she remained steadfast.

God's Unfailing Love was demonstrated once more, as after seven, gruesome, grueling months at the mental institution, Jonah was released.

It was a testament to the relentless faith and determination of a mother who refused to accept the status quo. Jonah stepped out of that place, a changed man, ready to face the world with newfound strength and hope.

CHAPTER TWENTY
THE SECRET PLACE

Matthew 6:6 NKJV

"But when you pray, go into your room, and when you have shut your door, pray to your Father who is in the Secret Place; and your Father who sees in secret will reward you openly"

Girlie witnessed the manifestation of her secret place in God, where she interceded for her son's release from the "crazy house." She prayed fervently for his mind to be renewed and made sound, just like Christ's.

She ran to the secret place!

She stayed in the secret place!

She travailed in the secret place!

She cried in the secret place!

She danced in the secret place!

She interceded in the secret place!

Because there is VICTORY in the Secret Place!

That Secret Place is not a position; but a PERSON!!

HIS FULL PRESENCE!!!

Girlie's faith and passion for Her Savior was rekindled as she bore witness to her answered prayers and God's Mighty Arm of Deliverance every single day!

Jonah was placed as an outpatient and had to be on constant medication that had him quite robotic.

Girlie wanted him to be released from such bondage, so she was in constant prayer for her son.

In her secret place.

For his freedom; to be unchained from every shackle.

Jesus died for his total man.

Mind, body and soul.

A sound mind, a healthy body and a restored soul. No way was Jonah going to be paying the price for his parents many misdemeanors!!

Not under her watch.

Slowly, but surely, Jonah was able to reintegrate into society, rejected initially, as he was labeled "mad man", but God supernaturally lifted him from that pit of depravity and shame. He was once again able to actively participate in life; not merely exist.

He regained his job, accepted back without any qualms or questions. It was a remarkable turnaround, something only God could orchestrate...

God's Love never ceases to amaze!!!

Jonah immersed himself in church and Bible studies. He became an evangelist, sharing and preaching at the highways and byways, telling everyone who had ears to hear of what God had done for him and the goodness of God that leads all to repentance!!

Girlie was overjoyed to see her son walking uprightly.

Choosing the Lord's Way.

Cindy, her daughter, was also thriving, actively involved in church activities like teaching Sunday School, and serving in the worship team with her husband.

Despite Roland's struggles with the drinking and partying, Girlie found solace in knowing that two out of three children were walking in faith. She held onto hope that her third child would also come to know Christ soon.

Girlie was at peace.

Jonah was delivered from insanity.

Because of the Secret Place she had with God!

CHAPTER TWENTY-ONE
NOT BY MIGHT NOR BY POWER....
BUT BY HIS SPIRIT

Zechariah 4:1(b)

"Not by might nor by power, but by my Spirit", says the LORD ALMIGHTY. *"What are you, O mighty mountain?"*

God manifested His Power and Presence, breaking through the mighty mountains of sickness and despair that lurked over His chosen ones, Girlie and Jonah.

His watchful eyes were upon them. His ear inclined upon them! Day and Night! His Word operational in their hearts and mind, performing miracles that seemed beyond belief.

Jonah flourished in both God's favor and his peers. He became an active member of his local church, anointing himself, before stepping out to pray for the lost, sick and broken. Witnessing the manifold glory, as people were saved, healed and delivered by the power of God.

His career also took a positive turn as a US-based company in Louisiana hired him, leading to frequent travels to the United States. Girlie rejoiced in her son's success, a stark contrast to his troubled past. She marveled at the answered prayers displayed before her eyes each day.

With newfound confidence and a buffed physique, Jonah became a magnet for attention, turning heads wherever he went. The once sickly child of Miss Girlie now walked as a miracle, drawing admiration from both near and far.

However, as Jonah's ego grew along with his muscles and bank account, pride began to find a place in his heart.

Cindy and Kenny welcomed a beautiful baby girl, named Rhona, bringing much needed joy, unity and strength to the family.

Unfortunately, the temptations of the world began to seep back into Jonah's life. Influenced by his offshore colleagues, he found himself slipping back into old habits of indulging in women and alcohol. Neglecting his prayer life and Bible reading, he started to avoid going to church, opting for "rest" at home instead.

One Sunday evening, near the Carnival season, Jonah was lured to a party at a prestigious resort in the area with his brother, Roland, Vishnu and a few other friends, were excited to mingle, hoping to meet new people, as this event were known to attract girls from near and far....

Jonah stood in a corner, puffing away at the cigarette in one hand and his mixture of 'brass and steel' in another, when suddenly his eyes dropped on the most gorgeous woman, he had ever laid eyes on.

His heart did a somersault and plunged to his stomach. Long, flowing black hair cascaded down her back, with a rounded derriere, not too huge but not small either.... he loved him some butt!!! It was his weakness....and her face, perfect.... God truly took His time with this one.... with her creamy complexion, Jonah felt love instantly....

I can marry this girl.... our children will be beautiful!!

He kept starring at her, absolutely mesmerized by her captivating looks and charm. She was the center of attraction; a quick glance around told him he was not the only man entranced by this beauty.

I have to make her mines! Jonah boldly declared to himself.

He mustered up the courage to walk over to her, as she threw her head back in laughter at something her girlfriend had said!

"Excuse me, miss", he managed to say, his heart pounding in his chest, "may I have this dance?"

She smiled broadly, revealing perfectly aligned white teeth, that radiated light leaving Jonah breathless. If he had doubts before, they vanished instantly as he knew for certain that she was going to be his wife....and oh would he cherish this beauty.... he had many other flings before, but none made him feel what this bombshell was evoking within him!

"Where did you come from, Mr. Hottie", she cooed softly, her voice sending shivers down his spine.

They moved rhythmically together on the dance floor, the music's beat fading into the background as Jonah's heart drummed loudly in his chest. With each passing moment he found himself falling deeper and deeper for this stunning woman named Paula.

Her name rolled off his tongue like a melody. Paula. She hailed from the capital city of Port-of-Spain; which didn't surprise Jonah. There weren't any girls in this sleepy village that looked anything remotely like her.

As they danced, they drew more than just curious glances. They were easily the best-looking couple not only at the party but in all of Trinidad, no doubt about it. They rocked the night away, lost in each other's embrace, as if they were the only two people in the world.

Jonah was in love!!!

CHAPTER TWENTY-TWO
MY TREASURE, MY BRIDE

Song of Solomon 4:10

Your love delights me, my treasure, my bride. Your love is better than wine, your perfume more fragrant than spices

Jonah and Paula's escalating, whirlwind romance became the talk of the village.

Girlie was shocked, and his family was aghast. It was evident to them that this relationship was based on lust and not Christ. Paula, though very young, was a woman of the world, not cognizant to the ways of the Lord. Despite being raised by Catholic nuns in a foster home, she lacked a Christ-like character and drew Jonah further away from his faith.

Within eight months, they were married, much to the chagrin of his mother and sister.

Cindy was livid.

She deliberated her brother was making a grave mistake, as Jonah, in her opinion, was not rooted and grounded in the Lord, always wavering in faith, not truly understanding what love was, and just wasn't prepared for the roles and responsibilities of a husband. Paula, on the other hand, with her lewd ways and limited intelligence, only wanted him as a trophy husband. In his lust, Jonah went ahead without the blessings of his mother and sister and married this young, beautiful but very immoral woman.

"He is going to regret this," were her churlish thoughts.

Jonah, moved Paula into an apartment on the outskirts of the village, as he didn't want his mother and wife to be living under the same roof, especially while he was offshore. He did not want any contention nor confusion.

He candidly told his mother, "Blessed is the child who has his own."

He firmly believed, that a married couple should leave and cleave, with no strings tied to any family members to hinder the marriage.

He and Paula lived blissfully at their place of residence. Jonah was truly happy with his bride; excitement mounting as he visualized his perfect life, with his perfect wife!

Jonah was totally enamored with his new bride, intoxicated with her beauty. He couldn't believe his good fortune in attaining such a prized possession. He missed her tremendously when he went to work and literally counted down the days until his return to her side.

Jonah and Paula wanted a large family! They allowed nature to take its course, eagerly starting the process of being 'fruitful and multiplying,' as described in Genesis 1:22.

After some time, rumors began to circulate about Paula's infidelity. People said she visited her ex-boyfriend and even spent nights at his home. There were also whispers of young teenage boys frequenting her apartment in Jonah's absence.

Girlie heard these rumors and voiced her concerns to her son, during one of his visits, but he dismissed them as vicious gossip.

He had the prize, and not many people were happy about that!

He scolded his mother for listening to and encouraging the gossipers, insisting that she should respect her daughter-in-law and be happy for his new life.

"Didn't you pray that I meet a good girl to settle down with?" he queried.

"Yes," his mother retorted, "but I just don't want any type of woman to be your wife, I prayed for a God-fearing woman, one who can pray and intercede for you. Who loves and values you. You are very special, Jonah and need a particular type of woman who truly cares about you and not the things that you can give to her."

"You are the prize, not her! Didn't you pay attention to what Sister Angela told you?" (Making reference to a counselling session he had with their pastor, Reverand Khan and his wife).

"You need a woman who understands you, who can pray for you, guide you, help you! Not someone who's been around the block a few times!" She cried.

Jonah was enraged.

"How dare you speak about my WIFE to my face like that! I love you, Mama, but that's enough of this nonsense! I truly love Paula, and she loves me. Very soon we will have a huge family as we both want lots and lots of children!! Either you accept that or not".

"If you cannot," he continued, enunciating each word for emphasis, "I will have no choice but to cut you off from our lives!"

Girlie flinched as if he had slapped her. After all she has been through with him up to this point in his life, for him to callously and casually cut her off from his life, as if she meant nothing to him stung beyond words!!

All she ever wanted was the best for Jonah! And this woman was only going to cause him pain and turmoil.

A trip that she feared he might never recover or come back from.

Paula was what one will term in local dialect, "pretty face but bad character."

Jonah stormed out.

He glanced back at his mother, the pain in his eyes mirroring the hurt in hers.

"Goodbye, Mama!"

CHAPTER TWENTY-THREE
KEEP HIM ALIVE

Psalm 41: 2(a)

The LORD will preserve him, and keep him alive; and he shall be blessed

Jonah felt sick!

What did he eat at dinner that was causing this ghastly feeling?

He ran for the umpteenth time to the bathroom as he became weaker and weaker with each passing moment.

By midnight almost half the men at camp were retching their stomachs out and the other half were having severe diarrhea. Pandemonium erupted as almost every offshore worker became deathly ill with some type of poisoning. The bosses and emergency medics were flown in via helicopter as they took charge of the situation to determine what had caused this mass food poisoning. Another crew of workers was also flown in, as the sick men were transported to the hospital.

Thankfully, Jonah was working at a local off shore camp and not the U.S.A. based one, so his beautiful wife could be with him. He was surely thankful that she was there at the hospital for him.

He was discharged shortly thereafter, as Jonah just wanted the warmth and comfort of Paula's arms. That was all he needed to recover from this horrible poisoning.

It was discovered that bad eggs were used in making eggnog beverages for the men that eventful night. The chefs and the catering company were fired immediately as gross negligence almost caused the death of over twenty men.

That was unacceptable.

However, Jonah was not responding well to the antibiotics and began deteriorating rapidly. His faeces were green and slimy, with an awful, pungent scent. He began dropping weight, way too quickly....

Somehow, Girlie had heard of this mishap, and rushed over to their apartment. She didn't care if Jonah had cut her off, she just knew that he needed her, as his featherbrained wife was absolutely clueless.

When she saw her son, she cried in horror. He was very thin and pale, his face drawn and skin hot to the touch, flushed and dry. He appeared severely dehydrated.

She scolded Paula for not attending to her husband as he evidently needed a doctor's urgent attention.

Paula quipped that he was taking his medication as prescribed by the doctor.

"Well, clearly it's not working and he needs emergency care," Girlie was irritated by his wife's flippant attitude.

Was she blind or just ignorant to these things?

Girlie admitted that though she too were not educated, at least she was blessed with a lot of common sense.

Paula, unfortunately had neither. Just a very pretty face, a voluptuous body with nothing else going for her.

"The only thing that girl knows to do is to have a good time and spend my son's money," she mused sardonically.

"Paula, please help me get Jonah dressed. I am taking him to the hospital" she commanded.

"You're not going to die! Not on my watch!" She declared to her bewildered son.

She hired a taxi as they sped towards the San Fernando General Hospital; where he was immediately hospitalized and treated for acute salmonella poisoning and dehydration.

The doctor advised Girlie, that because of her quick intervention, her son's life was saved; another couple of hours would have proven fatal for him.

She grew concerned.... his wife was right there.... watching him suffer and rapidly deteriorate.... didn't she care enough to ensure that he got the attention needed?

Girlie was extremely troubled by this revelation.

CHAPTER TWENTY-FOUR
CRUEL AS THE GRAVE

Song of Solomon 8:6 NKJV

Set me as a seal upon your heart, as a seal upon your arm; For love is as strong as death, Jealousy as cruel as the grave; its flames are flames of fire, a most vehement flame

Jonah was offshore in the U.S.A. trying to reach his wife on their recently installed landline, for the past hour, but it just kept ringing out.

Where could she be?

God, I pray she is, okay?

His lips curled in derision.

He hadn't prayed or thought about God since he met his wife.... Paula was his obsession, the one who ignited his very being! Woah! as he checked himself.

He was once on fire for God, and now the passion he had for this woman, quenched that blaze that he had lit for the Father!

She replaced the Lord in his life, compromising his beliefs to match her lack of faith.

His heart sank.

She finally answered the call, but by this time, it was close to midnight. She sounded flushed and disoriented. On his inquiry, she informed him that she fell asleep. He wanted to believe her, but his mother's burning words and the wagging tongues of the villagers, resonated in his ears.

They had been married for almost 5 years now, with not a sign of any babies in sight.... this was unnatural. Truth be told Jonah was afraid to discover the reason behind it.... was the fault his? Or Paula's?

Was she lying to him about not taking birth control pills? Here he was, over thinking again, as the thoughts swirled around his mind, tormenting him with a million different scenarios.

Jonah's mind was barraged with a kaleidoscope of thoughts that, yet again tormented him.

On his arrival back home, he began scoping around the house. What was he searching for? He had not a clue, but his spirit felt off, as if something was amiss, and he was not seeing what was right in front of his eyes.

Mr. Thomas, his next-door neighbor, almost got his head chewed off by Jonah that morning due to his nosy behavior and gossiping tongue. Mr. Thomas informed Jonah that there were two young fellows frequenting his home every time he was away working.

Jonah was agitated.

He loved this woman with every fiber of his being, his feelings for her were passionate and intense. He adored the sexual intimacy between them, and the thought of her being unfaithful and not matching his love and loyalty was something he did not wish to fathom.

He was rummaging through the kitchen and was drawn to the compartment beneath the stove. His face went white! The blood draining from his face.... his breath shallow and labored at what he found inside. Several pornographic magazines and VHS tapes were stashed neatly at the back.

WHY??

One thing he and Paula did not use were pornographic materials. They didn't need it. There was enough sexual energy between them to ignite a forest, and then some!!

"Sweetheart? Paula?" he called out. She was next door with her friend, Christine. He went outside and called her a bit louder.

She hurried over.

She truly was the perfect wife. She cooked for him. She was an awesome cook!! The house was always neat and tidy! She was obedient, never rude, loud or disrespectful. The sex was nothing short of amazing, but yet they lacked something......

Total honesty and transparency?

Jesus?

That third strand cord?

Paula was an atheist and did not want to hear anything about the Lord! Her traumatic experiences, together with the ongoing sexual abuse growing up with nuns, skewed her views about religion and God. She was dogmatic in her assertions that it was all a lie and façade to control people with their sinister hold over people's lives!

Jonah showed her his discovery.

She blushed as she told him that it served as a panacea to her, while he was away and offered her the comfort that she needed when he was at work. She missed him so much.

He somehow did not believe her. He told her as much.

She was offended as she assured him that nothing was happening outside of their marriage and that she was totally faithful to him. She loved him!!

Jonah was very unsettled in his spirit. It wasn't adding up and he was frankly fed up with the lies and gossiping tongues that had been plaguing their marriage from its inception. He wanted to believe her but somehow, he just KNEW!!

"What about the two young boys that always come over? I was told by Mr. Thomas that they are always here when I am at work."

She scoffed...

"That silly old bat just wants some of me…. jealous old fowl that he is….", "those boys are my cousins," she explained.

"So why have I never met them?" he asked aggressively.

Paula, was becoming uncomfortable with the way this conversation was going. Jonah appeared different somehow. She came up to him and flung her arms around his neck and cooed.

"Baby, you are over thinking again. Come let's go to bed and I can give you something to really think about."

Jonah unwrapped her arms, and pushed her gently away from him.

"Not now, Paula, I have lots to do before I fly back out to work again."

She starred at him with somber eyes.

The realization simultaneously dawned on them. He had only just returned home but was already making preparations to fly back out again.

True, he was an excellent provider; a diligent and dedicated worker, but that offered very little compensation for a warm, comforting body lying next to her nightly.

He saw her hurt, but offered no sympathy. She wanted the finer things in life, as she came from abstract poverty, hence the reason for her being raised by Catholic nuns.

She had expensive taste, and they were saving to buy a home. He hated renting and considered that to be dead money. He repeatedly told her that sacrifices had to be made, with him being the sole breadwinner, and was happy to work at every opportune moment. He wished she understood that.

Paula, unfortunately, did not.

CHAPTER TWENTY-FIVE
CRUSHED IN SPIRIT

Psalm 34:18

"The LORD is close to the broken hearted and saves those who are crushed in spirit"

Jonah had a sense of foreboding; as he flew in from Louisiana, devoid of the excitement he usually felt in returning to his wife. He and Paula hadn't spoken in two weeks; their relationship had deteriorated to such a point that they barely communicated while he was at work. He did not like this premonition that he had in his spirit that something was very wrong.

His fears were soon confirmed, as he entered the front door to be faced with an empty house!! Not one piece of furniture in sight. He called out to Paula, frantically searching for his wife.

"Paula," he screamed. "Where are you, honey?!"

It was more of a plea than a question. Jonah dropped to his knees in horror, as the implication dawned on him at what this meant!

He dialed 999.

"I want to report a kidnapping," he muttered in anguish.

Jonah refused to believe the obvious as he informed the officers that he came home from his work overseas to discover his wife missing, along with every single item in the house!!

The officers looked around. No forced signs of entry. Nothing to suggest a scuffle took place. They questioned the neighbors, but this one time they saw nothing.... the irony.

"Mr. Foster, are you sure someone kidnapped your wife.... or did she leave you?" was the question posed to him.

Jonah was shaken.

"No way, she did not leave me! That woman loves me and will never do me like that!" he just about shouted.

The officers looked at him with pity as he refused to come to terms with what was so obvious before him.

They left after dusting for fingerprints and a promise to have a full-scale investigation launched.

Jonah was inconsolable as he called his mother. He felt so ashamed at the way he had treated her, but she was the only person who understood.

Truly understood.

Girlie, hung up, as she hurriedly dressed to get to Jonah.

She called Kenny for a ride, too shaken to travel.

He and Cindy came over almost instantly. They had just bought a house in another village, Tabaquite. She had yet to visit them, as their family was growing with another girl, Kimberley, added to their lineup. Cindy had also insisted that her mother not trouble herself too much, as she met a girl who lived not too far from them, who was extremely helpful to her and assisted with Girlie's two granddaughters. Cindy constantly gushed about her new found sister/friend, Sherry Althea Armstrong.

Girlie broke out of her reverie, back to the reality that she was now faced with. She knew that this day would come. Paula was no good. Definitely not wife material for her precious son.

Now she was gone, taking all his furniture, and she was certain, money too!! She prayed that Jonah can get over this. His fragile heart was now broken into a million pieces; and she intended to be there for him at this crucial period.

Jonah moved back in with Girlie, his days and nights spent locked in his room, crying incessantly for a woman who betrayed his love and trust. Jonah took a month's sick leave as he was too distraught to function at his job.

When the dust had settled it was discovered that Paula was having extramarital affairs with various men in the neighborhood, initiating very young boys, and a boomerang for several ex-boyfriends, eventually leaving her husband for a man from her past that she appeared to have never gotten over. For someone so young, she had really been around a lot!!

Jonah was in absolute despair as each revelation unfolded, bringing with it more gut-wrenching pain than before. There was no reprieve as Jonah came to face to face with the harsh reality that his marriage, which he cherished and protected more than his own life, was now in shambles and irreparable. His treasure, turned to thrash!

He still had hopes of reconciliation, despite what she had done, so he ventured out one day to search for her. He found out, via her friend Christine, that she was living with her boyfriend about half an hour away, along with all the furniture that Jonah had bought for their marital home too!! All his sweat and hard work that he sacrificed to make her happy, was now being enjoyed with another man.

Unbelievable.

Jonah was taken aback at the cold, callous look staring at him through vicious eyes!! What did he do to her, for this type of treatment? He loved, cherished and cared for her the best he knew how; and this was the last thing he expected from his wife.

"I am never coming back to you, Jonah," was her heartless response to his impassioned plea for restoration. "Marrying you was a big mistake, and for what it's worth I am very sorry. We had a good time and you tried, but I need a man I can be with every night and who is there for me every day, not just every couple of weeks.... I have needs that you are incapable of meeting...." She trailed off as she saw the genuine brokenness in his eyes.

Jonah felt crushed in spirit, with each syllable spoken.

He drove back to Mayaro in utter despondency.

Days flew into weeks.

Jonah took extended leave from his job.

Jonah never left the house. His mother looked on in grief as she witnessed her son withering away daily, the light in his eyes now replaced with a darkness tainted with hatred. She had a premonition that Jonah may never be the same after this.

Paula filed for divorce and it was granted on the grounds of neglect and abandonment that she felt in her marriage due to his stringent work schedule. Jonah was alarmed at this allegation, as not once did Paula ever claim that she felt as such. She was always very happy to spend his money that this "stringent work schedule" afforded her. And now have the audacity to claim spousal support.

No way!!!!

She was living common-law with another man, and was not getting another penny from him, ever again. She had already wiped out their bank account and took every single item from their marital home to furnish the home she was residing in now. Hell no.... this b**** was not going to get away with what she was attempting....

Jonah was bitterly enraged by this preposterous turn of events. His once idyllic world, suddenly exploded, immersing him in its rampageous, charred rubbles.

Why Lord?

The divorce was finalized without any spousal support granted to Paula. Since they had no children together, and she had left him, taking most of the marital property acquired in their marriage, including the money in their joint bank account; the judge ruled that they were even. Paula had never worked and Jonah was the sole breadwinner. This decision was reinforced by the fact that she had moved in with a new 'husband.'

Jonah was shattered beyond repair. In that moment, he made two firm resolutions. He vowed never to allow himself to fall in love again like he did with Paula, his ex-wife. Additionally, he decided he would never get involved with another "red woman" ever again. To him, they were all "stink and dutty" and he wanted no part of such entanglements.

With a mixture of bitterness and disgust, he spat on the ground.

CHAPTER TWENTY-SIX
HEALING IN HIS WINGS

Malachi 4:2 (NLT)

"But for you who fear my name, the Sun of righteousness will rise with healing in his wings; and you will go free, leaping with joy like calves let out to pasture"

Jonah sought solace in drinking and partying, a futile attempt to escape the torment of his shattered marriage. Meanwhile, Girlie interceded for her son once more, feeling the extremities of his pain and urging him to seek the Lord for the healing that can only be found beneath His Wings.

Cindy, had another addition to her burgeoning family; a grandson, for Girlie, that brought much-needed joy after the recent calamitous events.

Candy, her "sister-in-law", Roland's common-law wife, also gave birth to a boy around that same time, further filling Girlie's heart with sheer bliss, that she was blessed with not one, but two grandsons almost side by side.

Amidst all this, Cindy continued to gush over her sister/friend, Sherry. However, she was not pleased that Sherry, like her brother Roland, was "shacking up" in a common-law relationship, with a guy from the area, and was now pregnant with her second child by him. She lectured to them that they needed to do the right thing. Eventually, after much pressure from Cindy, and a threat from Sherry that she will kill herself, Gregory Gomez agreed to marry her.

Cindy and Kenny, who were recently ordained as pastors, officiated their wedding, at the small church they both Shepherded in the area.

Despite his attempts to drown his sorrows in worldly pleasures, Jonah eventually decided he had enough of his self-destructive behavior. He made the choice to be baptized, feeling compelled to give his life back to the Savior.

It had been almost two years since his bitter divorce from Paula, yet Jonah still felt the lingering anguish. His heart, once full of love and trust, had hardened into stone. He reaffirmed to never love as deeply again, nor to be deceived by another "red woman," a term he now associated with deceit and betrayal.

Ever.

On the day of his baptism, the entire family gathered to witness this significant event in Jonah's life. Cindy, always the skeptic, cautioned Jonah of the importance of his decision.

"No more games with your salvation", Cindy informed him with her usual air of superiority, when addressing her siblings. She was so standoffish; especially now that she was Pastor Cindy.... Jonah was irritated by this and told her, in no uncertain terms, that she will always be considered his 'big head sister!'

For the first time, Jonah visited Cindy's home in Tabaquite, where the family gathered after Jonah's baptism, to have a 'lime.'

There, he met Cindy's sister/friend, Sherry Althea Gomez, recently married with two sons.

Jonah's nephew and nieces referred to her as Aunty Sherry.

The moment Sherry laid eyes on Jonah, she was totally smitten by this dashingly handsome man, with the dimple on his chin.

"Dimple on chin, devil within!"

She salivated at the thought.

Oh boy!

Why hadn't she met him sooner?

She would have never committed to Gregory. Why did Cindy never speak of her brothers? Especially this one that made her knees weak? God knows, she never felt this way before, and she had been around a few times, despite her quiet and shy demeanor.

He evoked such intense feelings within her that scared her!! She was a married woman, and had practically forced Gregory's hand in marriage. She and Cindy had clamored at him to make her an honest woman.... she regretted that so much now, and she dared not tell her friend how she felt, as Cindy would certainly disapprove of such adulterous emotions.

She felt herself longing for a man she barely knew.

Sherry camouflaged her inner turmoil with a smile as she courteously shook his hands as they were formally introduced.

Jonah, on the other hand was totally oblivious to her lustful thoughts, as he immediately saw her as family, because Cindy had introduced Sherry as her 'sister.' Sherry was not a good-looking woman, with a face that was as 'hard as banga,' he snickered.

Meanwhile, Jonah grappled with the constant tug-of-war between his spiritual convictions and the temptations of the world. He struggled to find balance, often feeling pulled in conflicting directions.

Then, one unexpected day, Jonah received a phone call.... from his ex-wife, Paula. She informed him that she had a daughter with the man she left him for, and she was facing troubles. Her 'husband' had thrown her out and she was relying on the goodwill of friends and family for shelter. Paula sheepishly asked if there was a remote possibility of reconciliation.

Jonah's response was a bitter laugh. He couldn't believe Paula had the audacity to ask after all she had put him through. He made it clear that reconciliation was out of the question, his heart now rigidly guarded against any further pain.

He hung up.

Did she actually believe that he was still that foolish, vulnerable man that would have done anything for her?

He laughed again.

Never, ever would he be a fool to any woman.... Especially those 'red' ones.... they were ALL so deceptive and dangerous....

She left him high and dry, having to work doubly hard to save again. She had taken a good chunk of his assets.... money that he had saved for a deposit on a home for them both....

At this point, working to accumulate money and moving ahead with his life were the most important things for Jonah.

As time passed, Jonah heard bits and pieces of his ex-wife's continued demise. Her ex-boyfriend also had his fair share of misfortune, losing both his legs to diabetes and was now living on the streets. Each piece of news brought a sense of dark satisfaction to Jonah's vengeful heart.

"That's for all the pain and anguish they both put me through," were his sinister thoughts.

Jonah had just returned from a three-month cycle from Russia, when the final blow came. Paula's sister, Carlene, called Jonah to inform him of the shattering news of Paula's passing.

She had died alone and broken, at the very young age of 28. Her daughter was now in foster care.

Paula died from an asthmatic attack, a shocking revelation for him, as during their time together, she never had any such attacks....so how did she become asthmatic? He was totally baffled by this news.

Jonah attended Paula's funeral, but not a drop of tear fell from his eyes. Instead, he felt a sense of vindication. The pain and betrayal he had endured had led to this moment; he stood over her final resting place with a heart blackened by bitterness and hatred.

As he left the funeral, Jonah couldn't help but feel a twisted sense of satisfaction. The dish of vengeance had been served, and he relished in the cold satisfaction of it all.

CHAPTER TWENTY-SEVEN
STOLEN WATER IS SWEET

Proverbs 9:17

"*Stolen water is sweet, and bread eaten in secret is tasty.*"

Jonah, found solace in the company of his nieces and nephew whenever he returned from his overseas work trips, always bringing back thoughtful gifts and souvenirs from the country he visited. Their presence eased his tormented soul, although he continued to grapple with the conflicting emotions that had become a permanent part of his personality. He was embittered and callous, aware that he was bound by anger and animosity, chained to the hurt inflicted by his now-deceased wife.

Unbeknownst to Jonah, Sherry had been harboring secret admiration for him. Each time she saw his vehicle pull up, she made it her business to find her way over to Cindy's house, donning the sexiest of shorts and tank tops that left very little to the imagination.

One day, when Cindy had to leave suddenly for church business, she left Sherry and her brother alone to babysit her children, along with Sherry's three sons, having a third child not too long ago.

Sherry looked Jonah straight in the eye, and boldly confessed her "crush" on him. Jonah was nonplussed, unsure on how to respond. She revealed that ever since she met him three years ago, she had carried a torch for him, its flames consuming her day and night.

"It's as if I can't get you out of my mind," she brazenly admitted.

Jonah was stunned. He had always seen her as family, referred to as "Aunty," by his nephew and nieces, with Cindy continuously affirming that Sherry was the sister she never had.

To alleviate the obvious tension and awkwardness of her admissions, Sherry offered to make him some of her special brew, a concoction of 'herbal tea,' that she whipped up occasionally.

She pointed out that he always seemed hyped and filled with anxiety; and this 'tea' was sure to relax him.

He graciously accepted her offer.... he was indeed very tense, his mind whirled in so many directions; the voices in his head returning to torment him, and peace would be so very much welcomed but, at this point, unattainable.

The tea was absolutely delicious, unlike anything he had tasted before. True to her word, it brought him a sense of serenity he had not experienced in a very long time. Overwhelmed with tranquility, he drifted into sleep on the couch as his eyelids drooped shut from weariness.

Jonah awakened to his sister and Sherry engrossed in conversation.

How long was he asleep?

He felt such peace.

He needed to always have that special brew.

He smiled.

He bid goodbye to Rhonda, Kimberley and his absolutely favorite person, his nephew, Randy. Ever since his birth, he was the real reason behind Jonah's frequent visits. Jonah kissed his sister, with a promise to return soon. Sherry, supplied him with a bottle of the specially blended 'tea,' with the assurance that there was plenty more of it, whenever he needed to 'relax.'

He thanked her and waved goodbye.

Just as Jonah had promised, he began frequenting his sister's home more often. Synchronously, his feelings for Sherry began to change. He began noticing her buxom behind and bursting bosom. Was she always this sexy?

"She's married, dude," he reminded himself sternly. That was a line he vowed not to cross, remembering the devastation caused by his wife's chronic infidelity, never wanting anyone to ever feel such hurt and pain. However, with each passing day, Sherry's sensuality became increasingly irresistible. It was a potent allure he hadn't felt since his days with Paula. Although he had been with women after his divorce, it was purely for instant gratification. He had sworn off developing any emotional attachments to another woman...ever again....

Upon returning from a work-related trip in Egypt, Jonah was relieved to be back home in Trinidad. It was long and drawn out and the extreme heat was unbearable. They had a special type of sun in that country. The sun in Trinidad felt cool in comparison and he was actually excited to be home!

Is that the reason for your excitement? The voice chided.

Rushing over to his sister's house, he hoped to see Sherry, thoughts of her consuming his mind during his time away. A yearning for her had developed, one that needed to be satisfied.

The affair between Jonah and Sherry was torrid and intense, a well-kept secret, that would have shocked their families. He was determined not to cause his mother any more pain, as her health was declining with each passing year, as the years of abuse suffered at the hands of his father was taking its toll on her frail, fragile frame.

Jonah felt an exhilarating high whenever he met with Sherry, the intoxicating feeling feeding his ego. They met at the various 'guest houses' across Trinidad, surreptitiously discreet in their indulging, clandestine rendezvous. It became their shared secret, and Sherry spared no effort in satisfying Jonah's every desires.

Jonah had her pledge her loyalty to him that despite her being married, they were exclusive to each other. Sherry assured him that that ship sailed a long time between Gregory and her, as he was constantly cheating on her and his latest conquest was her very own, much younger cousin.

Her answer delighted him.

She was an obsession to him....and Sherry was very pleased about that....

Fait accompli.

About a year into the adulterous, illicit love affair, Sherry shockingly discovered she was pregnant. Jonah was away at work, when she found out, and she knew she didn't want the baby. She already had three sons with her husband, Gregory and was content with that. She loved what she and Jonah had; only wanting to have a good time with her man, to be lavished with expensive jewelry, some of which he had gifted her from Egypt....22 karat gold!! and money, to which he was more than generous.

She didn't want any more children. Though Jonah had none of his own, she knew he would be ecstatic to have with her, as he had hinted on more than one occasion; it was not in her plan.

On his return, after a passionate reunion; she revealed her pregnancy to him; and as expected he was beyond excited.

"You know what this means, right?". Jonah exclaimed. "It's time for you to divorce that no good husband of yours so we can be a family."

Sherry eyes widened in uncertainty. Not sure how to feel about this sudden unexpected development.

When their sordid affair began, she knew what she wanted. Hot, luscious sex, with this eye candy of a successful, rich (in her opinion) man. Jonah was a drug, a man toy to have fun with, a riveting escape from her mundane marriage. Jonah DID all the right stuff, and it enthralled her to her toes!!

(Sherry, was what one will term a 'country bookie' ...and Jonah was a sophisticated man, traveling all around the world, who mesmerized her). He was the opposite of her boring and insipid husband, Gregory. However, the prospect of a scandal in her small village coupled with the thrill of their secret affair made her hesitant to make their relationship public.

She was content with the stolen moments and the excitement it brought. She never planned for their affair to become permanent, quite content with the thrill of the fling. However, Jonah's enthusiasm for their future together caught her off guard.

Unfortunately, Sherry lost the baby, after falling down a flight of stairs at her home. Jonah was away at work in the US for a 6-week project, which he had been called out to unexpectedly.

When he received the news, he was devastated; he accused Sherry of intentionally causing the miscarriage, citing her previous statement that she didn't want any more children. His suspicions and cold-heartedness resurfaced as the pain and despair that he had once felt with Paula's betrayal came washing over him once more. Pain, he thought was buried with his ex-wife, had now resurrected with new found anguish.

With Sherry, his once dormant feelings and passion resurfaced, feeling alive again.

When she informed him of their pregnancy, he was the happiest man in the world, as finally he would have a son or a daughter; someone to love him unconditionally.

He desired a huge family with Paula. Lots of children!!!

Unfortunately, she never bore him any, but went ahead and had a daughter with the man she eventually left him for.

Now, this wench had the audacity to lie to him, ripping his heart out with her callous and calm explanation of she 'losing' their baby.

He just knew that she had an abortion!!

She murdered his child.

Jonah could not overlook the betrayal and lies he perceived in her actions. He ended their relationship, deeply hurt and unable to forgive her.

He spent the next six months, immersed at work on a project back in the U.S.A.

CHAPTER TWENTY-EIGHT
STAND AT THE CROSSROADS

Jeremiah 6:16 NIV

This is what the LORD says: "Stand at the crossroads and look; ask for the ancient paths, ask where the good way is, and walk in it, and you will find rest for your souls". But **YOU** said, "We will not walk in it"

Jonah was indeed at the crossroads of his life. Sherry tried calling him, but each time he declined her call. He felt guilty about his involvement with a married woman, especially his sister's best friend, who, remained clueless of their illicit love affair.

Jonah sold his old car, and was looking to purchase a new one, but as he was seldom home, flying out every three weeks, he held off on making that purchase.

On one fateful day, while traveling from Mayaro to San Fernando, upon reaching Rio Claro, an exotic- looking woman boarded the taxi cab. His eyes lit up as her bronze skin and long, extremely neat dreadlocks captured his attention. She certainly was captivating, and that derriere was nothing short of spectacular. They exchanged phone numbers as she alighted with the promise to call.

Her name was Bernice, a single mom, with two sons and a daughter. They soon started an intimate relationship.

Jonah was hesitant to say anything to his mother, just yet, as Bernice's children were from three different men, which he knew would not please his mother!!

He tried to forget about Sherry and that relationship, not that he considered that an actual relationship; she being a married woman and the whole affair being shrouded in secrecy! He was getting older, and though he realized that his first and only love was Paula, he still wanted a family. It was his heartfelt desire to hear "Daddy" from his child's lips. He still felt the sting of the 'death' of the baby that Sherry 'lost!'

Jonah finally moved out from his mother's home, much to her displeasure. She was alone, never remarrying. Her health was not as it used to be, with a racking cough that persisted, which no type of medication was able to offer her relief. Jonah had already spent a lot of money carrying her to various specialists.

All in all, her faith remained steadfast, as she continually prayed for Jonah to find a good wife, to settle down and serve the Lord with a sound, stable mind. Cindy was doing very well, as she and her husband moved out from the Tabaquite area and moved to Cunupia, which was a huge transition, moving from a rural area to an urban community. They bought several properties, renting them out, and began pastoring a larger church. They were becoming very influential and affluent in wealth. Girlie was pleased about that.

Roland was still living with Candy and his only son, Braedan, never marrying each other. Roland was very much like his father, with the drinking and abusive behavior toward his common-law wife. Candy appeared to like that toxic treatment, choosing to remain in the relationship, despite the many brawling's and constant police intervention….to each his own.

Jonah was her main concern.

Jonah, by now, had moved in with Bernice, who wanted to buy the property in which she resided, but lacked the financing to do so. Jonah did not hesitate to buy the house, as he had been saving for some time now to finally buy a home, but somehow never found the right property to purchase.

He bought a brand-new car and Jonah started to feel like a responsible man again.

He and Bernice secretly married at the local courthouse. She was never so ecstatic in all her life and thanked her lucky stars for landing a successful man, who bought her a house and a car. Her children's fathers were no good bums, and she never had a man treat her so well. She bore children for three men and none respected or considered her worthy enough to marry her; she had resigned herself to her fate of remaining a spinster all her days.

Girlie was unaware of her son's secret antics until one day she demanded to know where he lived. He promised to pass by and pay her a visit. He wanted to surprise her with his new vehicle. He picked her up to carry her to lunch and she was excited to see him after many months.

"Where are we going for lunch, son?" she gushed in glee.

"Wait and see Mama," he said.

She glanced around in admiration, pleased that her son was doing well in life to purchase a brand-new vehicle out of the showroom. Her eyes dropped on a photo album. She reached for it, and was shocked at what she saw.

"Jonah???? You got married??" She questioned him, too horrified to say more than that!

Jonah chided himself for his forgetfulness at not removing the photo album from the back seat, as Bernice had taken it the day before to a friend's house to show off her beautiful dress and handsome husband. Bernice was the happiest woman on earth; her own home, a "rich" husband and new car!!!!

"Yes, Mama," he admitted with a hint of embarrassment.

His mother just looked at him, too mortified to even speak.

"Who is she? What's her name? Where is she from?"

She barely managed to say......

Of all the foolish things that Jonah has done, this has got to take the cake!!

He proceeded to explain about their meeting, short courtship, and impulsive wedding.

Impulsive was not the word that his mother had in mind....

Jonah reluctantly carried his mother to his new home, to which Girlie, told herself that there was no longer anything that Jonah can do to shock her any further.

She met Bernice and immediately disliked her, though she did not display that sentiment. She hid her feelings from both Jonah and Bernice, his new 'wife.'

Just wait until his sister hears about this....my oh my.... She will be infuriated!!!

Girlie was so disappointed in Jonah.

He was smart for men, but stupid for women, she often told him; whose gender somehow seems to manipulate him into foolish and immoral behavior.

He is a man of God. She prophesied.

After God's own heart. Was her bold declaration.

That was her constant prayer. And for him to find a good wife and obtain FAVOR from the Lord!! It seemed the more she prayed, the more rebellious Jonah became. He liked doing his own thing, going his own way, not wanting to be told what to do. He was wrong and strong.

Father, please help your son! This is his second wife, and another femme fatale that will bring him serious calamity and pain!

"A guarded heart is wise and scriptural. It keeps out negative people. A hardened heart, though, will silence the voice of the Holy Spirit."

Steve Sauceda

Jonah's heart was not guarded, but hardened……

CHAPTER TWENTY-NINE
YOUR MOTHER'S TEACHING

Proverbs 1:8 -9

*Listen, my son, to your father's instruction **(God)** and do not forsake your mother's teaching, they are a garland to grace your head and a chain to adorn your neck"*

Jonah had just returned from another project in Egypt; exhausted to the marrow, as he was literally out in the parched desert for five grueling months. He did not particularly like that country as the sun was scorching, and its angry rays was even felt in the blistering heat of the night. He did miss his wife, albeit not how it used to be with Paula, which was a longing akin to obsession, but he made good on his promise to himself to never let another woman capture and captivate his heart like his deceased ex-wife.

His phone rang. It was his personal banker. That's odd, Mrs. Ferguson doesn't usually call unless it's an emergency or to relate the latest investment scheme offered by the bank.

She told him, after exchanging the formal pleasantries, that one of his accounts, the Money Market Investment Fund, was depleting rapidly and he needed to replenish it as soon as possible to continue the benefits of its excellent interest rates.

He was flabbergasted.

He never withdraws any money from that account. He hung up, with the assurance that he will come in personally to check on it.

He had a sinking feeling in the pit of his stomach. It's been three years since he and Bernice were married, and life was good. Not great, but good. Deep inside he felt empty and miserable, but he camouflaged it perfectly and drowned himself at his job.

He worked assiduously to provide for his family. Bernice was unable to bear him any children, as he had learnt, **after they had tied the knot**, her tubes were tied after she had her last daughter, believing she was going to be single forever.

This delayed bit of information, troubled him, as he felt that should have been divulged before the marriage, nevertheless, he took care of her children as his very own.

His mother had distanced herself; Bernice made her feel uncomfortable, on the few occasions that Girlie visited, and Bernice made it plain that she wasn't going to the 'bush' to visit any family member. Jonah had mixed feelings. On one hand, he was happy about that because he sensed that she was disappointed in him and his choices in life. On the other, he truly missed his mom, and her witty words of advice. She was a very wise woman despite her lack of formal education. His sister withdrew too, as on hearing of his rushed, secret wedding, decided it was the last straw and cut him off as well.

Sherry made several attempts to call him, but he declined every time. He was certain that she had heard of his nuptials through his sister. So why couldn't she just move on? She was married and so was he. Nothing good could ever come from that...just hot and raunchy sex....

Bernice had indicated to him earlier, that on his return, she wanted to reverse the procedure of tubal ligation, as she decided that she wanted to bear his children; to which Jonah readily agreed. His heart sang as the prospect that he could finally be a father.

The next day, on his visit to the financial institution, it was discovered that his wife had taken out a hefty chunk of the money and opened a separate account on her and her firstborn son's names!

Jonah almost freaked out! What the hell!!??

The figures, however, did not add up, as what was taken from the account did not reflect the missing sum. What did she do with the balance of his money?

Apparently, his wife, while he was away, slaving at his job, flew out to New York with her children to visit her siblings and mother, spending lavishly to the envy of her family.

Jonah began questioning the validity of his marriage; did this woman truly care about him? Or was it only about her wants and needs?

Jonah was truly heartbroken.

He confronted his wife, who denied that was her intentions, and made up the lame excuse that she transferred the funds in case of his demise, which did not make sense whatsoever to him. The argument escalated to the point that her teenage son got involved, and he and Jonah physically fought. Jonah refused to be disrespected in his own house, and kicked him out.

Bernice was devastated.

That was the beginning of woe and sorrows in their marriage, as all that was done came to light. Jonah regretted his marriage, as his mother's words came back to haunt him.

"You need a woman who understands you. Who can pray for you. Guide you! Help you!"

"I just don't want any woman as your wife, I prayed for a God-fearing woman, one who can pray and intercede for you. Who loves and values you. You are very special, Jonah and need a particular type of woman who truly cares about you and not the things that you can give to her".

Jonah wanted so badly to turn back time, right about now. He only ever wanted peace, and all he had in his life was chaos and turmoil. His phone rang, startling him out of his deep thoughts....

It was Sherry.

He stared at his phone, tempted to answer....

He declined the call. He wanted to make his marriage work, despite its tumultuous turn of events.

He no longer trusted his wife, and took her name off all his accounts, giving her just enough cash to sustain the regular bills and household expenses. He was called out to work unexpectedly, to Alabama, so Jonah, went ahead and paid for the procedure to reverse the tubal ligation. He determined that this was ideal as Bernice could heal from the minor surgery and on his return, start working on building their family....at least there is light at the end of this very dark tunnel.

So, he thought!!

A year had passed, and Bernice was still unable to conceive. Which appeared odd, as they both followed all the necessary rules. Timing of ovulation, and keeping his swimmers at optimum level.... Bernice feigned ignorance to why they failed to get pregnant. Another year flew by, to which Jonah took three-month sabbatical, determined that during that time frame, he would impregnate his wife....to no avail. Jonah became frustrated as the more he tried, the greater the failure.

Unknown to his wife, Jonah decided to visit the clinic where Bernice had her procedure done, resolute in his mind to source the problem.

Maybe the reversal somehow failed. After paying so much money, he needed answers.

The receptionist was very helpful, flirtatiously batting her eyes as she stared at him hungrily, but Jonah was too upset to pay her any attention.

To his utter shock, Jonah discovered that the tubal ligation reversal procedure his wife had promised to undergo was never done. It was a jarring realization that struck him like a bolt of lightning. Questions raced through his mind, each more bewildering than the last.

WHY!!! He exclaimed loudly in his head, the frustration and disappointment echoing in his thoughts.

In that very moment, standing in the clinic's sterile waiting room, Jonah felt the foundation of his marriage crumble beneath him. It was a betrayal of trust, a breach of their vows that cut deeper than any physical wound. The revelation marked the beginning of the deterioration of his marriage to Bernice.

The uncertainty of her motives, the lies and deceit unraveling before him, left Jonah reeling with a mixture of anger, confusion and heartache.

CHAPTER THIRTY
MORE THAN YOU CAN CHEW

Job 13:14

"*I am biting off more than I can chew, and taking my life in my own hands*"

Jonah's home became a living nightmare after he discovered his wife's duplicity. Instead of showing remorse for her blatant lies and deceit, gaslighted her husband, accusing him of deception and betrayal, for sneaking around behind her back to shame and embarrass her name at the clinic.

It was a shocking revelation for Jonah. He learned that instead of the tubal ligation reversal, Bernice had undergone an abdominoplasty. He chided himself for his ignorance, realizing now the signs he had missed. Her toned stomach and sudden fashion choices, and obtaining a naval ring should have been red flags. He recalled a conversation with a mutual friend that his vehicle was seen regularly at a very popular 'obeah man's' resident. He wondered if she had used witchcraft to ensnare him into marriage.

Did she 'dirty' her hands to ensure that he married her? Have him to be a doting, hardworking husband, who worked while she played? Was she only using him for his money and status? On many occasions, he heard the buzz that she never fully broke it off with her daughter's father…. but he foolishly brushed it off as slander and village banter.

His trust shattered; Jonah felt nauseated at the thought of being used once again by a woman.

The realization of her betrayal stung deeper than he could have imagined.

How could he face his mother, having cut off all familial relationships to please his wife.

Clearly, Bernice had become vindictive as Jonah had taken her name off all his various bank accounts and limited her spending by giving her a monthly stipend.

Life in his house became unbearable. Bernice became argumentative and vexatious in spirit, withholding intimacy and neglectful of her wifely duties.

Jonah, casting his pride aside, finally confided in his mother, who advised him to leave before things escalated to violence. But Jonah, proud and determined to stand his ground, refused to budge.

He dismissed such a ludicrous thought; leave his house? That's his house, and that Jezebel was not going to force him to leave.... he bought that property with blood, sweat and tears!! While she's been running around playing the harlot, he was working 12-hour graveyard shifts, so that they can live a very comfortable life.

NOT HAPPENING!!

Relief came when he was called away for work to Russia for three months. At least he would be away from the constant bickering, and nagging that became his daily bread.

During this time, his only solace were the prayers of his mother and the counsel of his friend, Vishnu. But even from afar, the troubles at home haunted him. He no longer spoke cordially with Bernice, so he never bothered to call her. His mother indicated that a car was constantly seen parked not too far from his gate, so much so that the neighbors began speculating that Bernice had a nightly visitor.

Girlie implored her son, that she wanted him out of there, as Bernice had family members belonging to gangs and she feared for his life. Anxious for his safety, she implored him to leave and return home.

Jonah hated what he was doing to his mother.

She had been through so much, and here he was adding fuel to her misery. How could he ever forgive himself? His life was a tattered tapestry of mental turmoil caused by his many cataclysmic choices in life. His pattern of behavior had resulted in long term negative consequences. He wished he can have a 'do over' with his life.... how differently life would have been had he listened to his mother.

With a heavy and despondent heart, Jonah returned from work, feeling lost and desolate. He did not want to be hypocritical and turn to the Lord, where for years he had neglected fellowship with the Holy Spirit. He knew that he was heading to a dark dungeon of despair, spiraling out of control. In a moment of desperation, he called out to God for help, feeling the crushing weight of his mistakes descending him further into sinking sand!

Jesus, take the wheel!! As I have done a lousy job with my life!

I have crashed this vehicle too many times! Please drive this vehicle for me! He barely mustered.

He knew he had strayed far from the path his mother had hoped and prayed for him.

As if on cue, another one of Sherry's persistent calls flashed on his phone.

This time, he answered....

They rekindled their affair; Jonah was desperate for validation and Sherry was the healing balm he needed.

He found comfort and passion in her arms. She offered him the sanctuary he needed in the midst of his chaotic life, and Sherry reiterated her love and devotion to him, in their intimate pillow talks. But this flaming affair only added fuel to the inferno at home. Bernice, suspicious and jealous, accused him of infidelity, igniting explosive arguments and threats.

After one such tempestuous disagreement, Jonah, called his mom, who begged him to come back home, as her doors were always open to him. Jonah wrestled with his choices, knowing he had once again veered off course.

"Jonah, I fear something drastic is about to happen, nothing good can come out of this, please, son I beg you, just leave that mess and come home".

Girlie was grieved and worried, her health deteriorating even further.

She begged God to help her son, as this time, it would appear that her impetuous son had bitten off more than he can chew!

CHAPTER THIRTY-ONE
YOUR OWN WICKEDNESS

Jeremiah 2:19 NKJV

"Your own wickedness will correct you, and your backslidings will rebuke you. Know therefore and see that it is an evil and bitter thing that you have forsaken the LORD your God, and the fear of ME is not in you" says the LORD GOD OF HOSTS

Jonah had just returned home from washing his vehicle. His wife was nowhere to be seen, so he assumed she was out with the children.

His phone rang. It was Sherry. His heart sang with excitement at her voice; he hadn't heard from her for a few days!! A smile played at the corners of his lips, as he went into the bedroom, lounging on the bed, speaking sensually to each other, promising to rock each other's world with their next planned meetup.

"I can't wait to see you, babe." Jonah drooled; his anticipation palpable even over the phone. "That insipid, cold fish wife of mine could never satisfy me as you could. I would forever love you, Sherry," he continued, totally lost in the moment.

Little did he know, Bernice had been hiding under the bed, her heart pounding with a mixture of dread and fury as her suspicions were confirmed. Jonah was having an affair. She had his conversation with that whore recorded. He would be unable to deny this in court as her intentions was to take him for everything he had!

Bernice flew out from underneath the bed. Jonah was aghast, as he faced the fury of his belligerent wife, as she screamed and cursed, slapped and bit him, not caring in the heat of the moment, as realization hit that her marriage was over and the intense pain of betrayal she felt in her heart.

"I will kill you, and bury you and take every penny you have," she threatened, her voice a mix of desperation and anger as she grabbed his phone and flung it against the wall, shattering it into pieces.

Jonah was stunned, his mind reeling from the sudden turn of events. Anger rose within him like a tidal wave.

"I will kill you first before I allow a slut like you to take away what I worked so hard for!!! You work on your back for all types of men, every last one of them refused to marry you, using you for their temporary relief." Jonah's voce thundered with fury, his eyes blazing with anger.

"But you fooled me, made me believe you would carry my child, deceiving me, knowing full well, you had your tubes tied, stealing my money and entertaining your ex-lovers while I toil to put food in your mouth. Fattening you, so you can go whoring all over the place, while I work like a jack a** for you and your bastard children! Don't test me, woman. I will chew you up and spit you out!!" He bellowed, beside himself with fury!!

Who the hell did she think she was!!

He stood there, seething with rage. He looked at his phone, shattered beyond repair!! The weight of betrayal and deceit bore down on him like a heavy burden, as he struggled to comprehend the depth of her hypocrisy.

He glared at his broken phone, a symbol of the shattered trust between them. Bernice's piercing screams filled the air as she frantically tore off her clothes, her actions erratic and wild. Without a second thought, she bolted out of the house, stark naked, her voice echoing through the neighborhood as she cried for help.

Jonah stood there, dumbfounded by her sudden outburst.

Help? From what?

The red, angry marks of her nails etched into his skin, a painful reminder of the chaos that had just unfolded.

Has she gone mad? He was shocked at her behavior!!

He hurriedly followed after her, his cheeks burning with embarrassment at the thought of what the neighbors might be witnessing.

As he caught up to her, he wrapped his arms around her trembling, naked form, trying to shield her exposed body from prying eyes. Hot tears streamed down her cheeks, as she continued to wail in anguish, her cries piercing the night air.

"What's wrong with you, Bernice!? You started this whole mess!" Jonah's voice a mixture of frustration and disbelief. "And now you're running out here naked, screaming for help, pretending to be the victim? Unbelievable!"

Through her sobs, Bernice managed to choke out her words, her eyes filled with hurt and betrayal. "Jonah, how could you do this to me? Who is this tramp that you're pledging your love to?"

Her accusation hung heavily in the air, the weight of her words sinking deep into Jonah's already troubled heart. Bernice was inconsolable at the prospect of Jonah's apparent infidelity. She collapsed onto the couch, her body trembling and spent.

Jonah, feeling a mix of guilt and confusion, ventured back into the bedroom hoping to salvage his broken phone. The room felt heavy with tension, the air thick with the remnants of their explosive argument. It was clear that things had taken a dangerous turn, and it was best for them to be separated for a while. On the other hand, he knew that Sherry was probably worried sick, having been privy to some of the chaos through their conversations.

As Jonah settled down on the bed, his mind whirling from the events of the day, he was utterly exhausted and emotionally drained. The weight of the situation pressed heavily on his shoulders, each breath feeling like a struggle against the turmoil within him.

Suddenly, the quiet of the room was shattered by the loud, heavy footsteps of three well-built police officers. Their presence was commanding as they barged into the bedroom.

Without a word, they swiftly closed the distance to Jonah, their movements precise and efficient. With surprising force, they grabbed him off the bed, their strong hands gripping him firmly. Jonah was caught off guard, his body jerking in their grasp as they handcuffed him with a practiced efficiency.

The room spun around him as he was forcibly pulled to his feet, the officers towering over him like imposing giants. The suddenness of their arrival left Jonah stunned, his mind struggling to process the swift turn of events.

In that moment, Jonah felt powerless and vulnerable, a mere pawn in the hands of the law. The air crackled with the tensions as the officers tightened their hold on him, their expressions grim and unwavering.

"Mr. Foster, you are under arrest", one of the officers barked, his voice bursting with authority.

Jonah's mind raced, his heart pounding in his chest as he tried to make sense of the situation.

"What? Why!" he protested, his confusion evident in his voice.

"Your wife called us," another officer explained, his tone stern. "She said you threatened and beat her, running her out of the house in the nude. Now she's traumatized and extremely fearful for her life!"

Jonah's shock was palpable. "I didn't touch her!" he protested, his voice raising in disbelief, at the blatant lies concocted by his wife.

How could he beat her?

He didn't touch her in any aggressive manner.

This whole fiasco was beyond bizarre!

Where were her bruises, if he did indeed beat her?

Just then, Bernice appeared in the doorway, red-faced with blood oozing from her mouth. She had scratches, bruises and contusions all over her body. A stark contrast to the woman Jonah had left on the couch, just an hour ago.

WHO DID THIS TO HER????

Did she do this to herself?

Did someone do this to her, to frame him?

Jonah was so confused and angry at this crazy sequence of events!!

Bernice cried hysterically, "I don't want him back in this house, please, he might kill me next time. He said he will chew me up and spit me back out!! PLEASE, I don't want this man near me, ever again!" She wailed even harder.

"Ma'am, please pull yourself together! I will advise you to go to see a doctor, and carry the report to the courthouse tomorrow morning and apply for a restraining order, and he will not be able to come anywhere near you," the officer advised her.

She maliciously smiled at Jonah, as the officers jerked Jonah away from the bedroom.

Jonah was too numb to speak or think as the unfathomable faced him.

This wicked woman planned this all along. She only ever wanted this house, and now he was being forcibly evicted out of his own home that he worked so very hard to buy.

Father, I cannot believe this is happening to me. Were his anguished thoughts.

This was a diabolical plot, with the malicious intentions to legally pursue his other assets. He needed to think fast. How could he get out of this messy situation?

Jonah bowed his head in shame and despair, the neighbors looking on in curiosity, as the officers, whisked him away.

How could he have been so blind? Fallen into this ensnaring trap. Jonah's eyes welled in tears, at the anguish felt once more at the hands of another wife's utmost betrayal shattered him.

CHAPTER THIRTY-TWO
MANY ARE THE AFFLICTIONS

Psalm 34:19

Many are the afflictions of the righteous, but the Lord delivers him out of them all

Jonah, once again, moved in with his mother. She truly was a remarkable woman! He promised himself, that another female would never again place a wedge of contention, between him and his dear praying mother. Jonah was fully aware that he was in deep hot water, and it would take another miracle from God to rectify this situation -a situation which he brought upon himself, hook, line and sinker. Did God have this much patience with him, to unravel this disaster that Jonah bought with his own hands?

Bernice filed for divorce on the grounds of abuse, both verbal and physical, and adultery; and true to Jonah's prediction, began pursuit of his assets. She wanted the car, half of the money in all his accounts, both local and US, and half his monthly earnings. And the house!

Girlie and Cindy were infuriated by the audacity of this venomous snake posing as a battered housewife. Girlie, unfortunately had very little fight left in her, growing weaker as the days progressed, exacerbated by the arrest of her son. Grief and anxiety were her constant companion of late, especially where Jonah was concerned!

Meanwhile, Cindy came up with a plan. No way was this Delilah going after her brother's assets. Yes, she may dislike his choices, but he was family, and no wicked witch was going to get away with such covetousness!!

Cindy coerced Jonah into agreeing to sign over all his money and title to his vehicle, between herself and a member, of Cindy's church, Faith, a trusted friend and deacon of the church, who readily agreed with the plan. Jonah would sign over everything to them; leaving nothing to his name. When the lawyers inquired of Jonah's assets, it would be the bare minimum. Unfortunately, he couldn't do that with the house, as that would raise a huge red flag, so he could only hope for the best.

The trial was messy, with Bernice citing Jonah as having an affair all throughout the marriage, his financial abuse, leaving her with little to no money whenever he left for work, sometimes for months on end, leaving she and her children suffering. And the constant, relentless beatings suffered at his hands!!

It was all a blatant lie!! Yes, the truth was out, he was having an affair, but only after she stepped out of line, her affairs with her exes, stealing his money and duping him with so many lies. The omission of her sterility!! He never once laid hands on that woman!! Pure evil, that's what she was!!

In the court documents, Sherry Althea Gomez was labelled as the woman having the adulterous affair with her husband, causing the death of their marriage, evidenced by the voice note of Jonah pledging his undying love and devotion to Sherry, as he made the disparaging comment about 'his cold fish of a wife;' (the recording she had taped of their conversation, while she hid under the bed) together with the photos of her bruises from his "alleged" brutal assault.

Cindy was shocked that her sister/friend was named as one of the reasons for the breakdown of his marriage! Not that she considered it a marriage, but she could not believe that her brother and "sister" were having an affair. She knew her, or thought she did. Sherry revealing a side to her that she never believed existed. She falsely adorned herself as a 'good Christian woman,' devoted to God, her husband and children; never loud or boisterous, with a calm and humble spirit. Cindy was still reeling with disbelief. Cindy had confided some of her own dark secrets to Sherry; things her husband and children must never be privy to!!

Lord, have mercy!

Both Sherry's and her children were so close, akin to siblings!! Cindy tried in vain to come to terms with Jonah and Sherry's relationship. They were lovers for years! She turned beet red in righteous indignation!! The lies and deceitfulness were too much to bear!!

Jonah learnt that Bernice had gone to Gregory to make him aware of the ongoing extramarital relationship, between his wife and her husband. She related her ordeal to everyone who would listen, slandering Jonah and Sherry every moment she got.

It was juicy gossip in Tabaquite and Mayaro. Bernice, even visited her "spiritual" house and threatened Sherry that she would die soon. Bernice was acrimoniously vengeful, seeking restitution by any means possible.

Girlie Foster's health continued to decline.

Jonah, who was previously wrapped up in his own world with the many problems surrounding him, realized what was happening to his mother. She needed urgent care and attention!! He prayed that it wasn't too late!

Her persistent cough together with acute body pains, left more questions than answers. She was not responsive to any medication or treatment rendered. She complained of agonizing pain in her chest, arms and thigh muscles with difficulty breathing, becoming very feeble and weak, barely able to walk.

Jonah did not know which was worse - the embittered battle with a woman out to get back at him for her perceived hurt, or the desperate battle to get the care and treatment needed for his dear mother- his lifeline, his pillar of strength and the only woman who truly cared for him, unconditionally.

Lord, please don't let my mother die.

"I was so taken up in my messed-up life that I have neglected my own mother." He thought in regret.

Each specialist, came up with various diagnoses. It was determined by one that she needed immediate hospitalization!

Jonah was so broken.

His divorce was finalized, two weeks later, with Bernice being granted the marital home. She however, received no alimony or other assets due to Jonah's sister's wisdom, in turning the tables on his avaricious ex-wife!

The charges of assault and battery were also dropped because of the inconsistency of Bernice's testimony, and the representation of the best lawyer in the country. Jonah was grateful as those serious charges could have sent him to prison for a few years!

Jonah continued seeking solace in the welcoming arms of Sherry, as they had mutually decided to continue their relationship; as everything was already out in the open, "so let the chips fall where it may." At the very least, he was not going through this dual ordeal alone....

Sherry wanted to visit his mother, he wasn't sure that was such a good idea, as he knew from a previous conversation that she did not approve of their affair.

Sherry insisted, so Jonah relented.

On that fateful Sunday, they both proceeded to pay his mother a visit. His heart sank, when he saw his sister at her bedside.... wasn't she supposed to be at church?

Cindy ignored him, and addressed Sherry.

"What are you doing here?!" Cindy shrieked. She looked at her former 'sister' in scorn, noticing her very tight, short pants and revealing top. Love bites in abundance all over her neck and chest....

These people have absolutely no shame.

Why did Jonah bring her here! Mammy explicitly told him that this relationship would carry him down another dark, dismal hole....as if he needed more of that! His choices in women left them all baffled.... the dirtier the reputation, the more appealing to her brother.

Lord, help this boy....

Jonah did not stay long. He bade his hasty goodbyes to his mother, who was too weak to barely utter a syllable, yet the look she gave him spoke volumes.

The next day, Jonah, riddled with guilt, visited her again.... alone.

The doctors were in with her, so he decided to look around. He peered into the adjacent room, his eyes widening as he saw a "sweet looking reds" at an older gentleman's bedside. He was a huge, giant of a man, the bed a bit too small for his bulky frame. She appeared distraught and looked deep in prayer as she held his hand.

"Hmmm," he thought, "she has a glow about her, almost angelic!"

"Hey," he checked himself.... "No more 'red' woman for you. They're all bad news." Still very much pained by the intense betrayal of his dead ex-wife!!

"Bernice, and the other women you had hooked up with over the years were not 'red,' and each one caused you immense pain, so what's your point?" A voice corrected him immediately.

I am not going down that pathway again.

He decided that he and Sherry were moving toward a permanent relationship. He had forgiven Sherry for the 'loss' of his child, as they mutually agreed they will continue trying.

The doctors' prognosis was grim. They hadn't much hope for his mother, as the latest test discovered a thoracic growth in the back of her throat, seriously inhibiting breathing, so much so that she had to be placed on oxygen. It was also revealed that the aches and pains in her body were caused by polymyositis; and it was already in an advanced stage and her body became too weak for continued treatment.

She looked at her son, tears streaming out of the sides of her eyes.... she knew she was dying, the racking pains in her body paling in comparison to the ache in her heart for Jonah, her precious first-born son. Leaving him in peril, juxtaposed between two immoral women that had the capacity to potentially destroy him. She hoped her prayers will follow him and have its victorious expected end even beyond her grave.

She trusted her Father. Jonah will someday meet his perfect match...his helpmeet, his rib and flesh of his flesh, his kingdom wife who would do him good all the days of his life, and be a crown unto his head. He would meet and marry that woman who would understand and love him despite his many failures and mistakes.

Jonah, too stunned to grasp the gravity of the doctor's revelation, as his heart ached for his mother; who lay their dying, no amount of his money able to cure or help her.

He saw she was tired.

Battle weary.

She fought the good fight of faith; a true soldier. She was prepared to cross over. Into the Loving Arms of her Lord; whom she served diligently most of her life!

He saw it on her face, as an overwhelming, celestial presence surrounded her.

"Rest, Mama," he whispered.

Jonah was devastated.

NOTHING prepared him for this moment!!

CHAPTER THIRTY-THREE
MY SOUL FINDS REST

Psalms 62:1-2

My soul finds rest in God alone; My salvation comes from HIM. He is my rock and salvation; He is my fortress; I will never be shaken.

Girlie Foster was laid to rest at Bristol Public Cemetery in Mayaro.

Jonah was numb and dumbstruck, unable to come to terms with the fact that he had just buried his precious mother, dug her grave and covered it himself, solely funded by him. Both his siblings claimed to have no money for her burial, which he knew were lies, especially coming from his sister, who he knew was rolling in wealth! He was grateful to her for keeping his money and assets safe from his greedy ex-wife, but Cindy always opposed him, insulting, ridiculing and belittling him throughout his life, with an air of superiority, looking down her 'snotty' nose at everyone! No humility whatsoever!! She brought the title of pastor into serious disrepute! His sister and brother-in-law were only fooling themselves!!

He broke out of his reverie; His heart was overwhelmed with pain for his beautiful, prayerful mother who was now GONE!!

How his soul was in agony, no longer able to hear her witty advice, which he had often ignored and brushed aside most of his life!! A woman, whose tears and prayers had kept him alive. Roland wailed and Cindy bawled in grief and anguish, each feeling the pain, of losing their beautiful, virtuous mother.

Her children surely arose and called her blessed. Proverbs 31: 28(a)!

Jonah was grief stricken, yet, not shedding a tear, his heart calloused and cold; a defense mechanism he had adopted since the devastating breakup with his wife, Paula.

Jonah pondered at his tempestuous life! His journey; feeling like the biblical Jonah, except the cyclical storm and whale perpetually swallowed him, regurgitated by his many blunders and mistakes.

He can hear his mother's words.

Jonah, you are smart for man, but stupid for woman!

How he missed his mother, the wound fresh at her sudden passing at the age of 65.... ironically the year of his birth... (19)65.

Did the right woman for him even existed? Were there even any good ones left?

Sherry gradually grew distant, making up excuses as they barely interacted. Ever since his divorce, she apparently lost interest in continuing the relationship. Jonah spent his days and nights in solitude, at his mother's house, agonizing over his turbulent life. He had continued living with his mother, after being forcibly ejected from his own home. Bernice received a debt-free house in the divorce settlement, as he had paid off the mortgage prior to the violent eruption with his ex-wife.

Not another woman, would ever do him dirty again. He promised himself, a grim look etched on his face.

His heart further hardened, devoid of emotions. He perhaps needed to seek God, and God alone, then everything else might fall into place. His pursuit of peace had eluded him every single time, and now it was time for him to seek the Source of Peace and not just an attribute of it.

Jonah decided to 'try' Jesus again, as he fell on his face in repentance, completely spent by life's brutal assault.

One Sunday afternoon, his sister and brother-in-law visited him as he was packing his suitcase to fly out for work the next day. He hadn't seen them since their mom's funeral a few weeks ago. Jonah was glad to see them, as within the recent weeks he meant to remind Cindy to begin the process of transferring his assets back to him.

As he was just about to do so, Cindy threw something at him. It looked like a legal document.

"What is that?" he queried.

"Look at it, you're not blind, so read it," She responded, in her usual uppity air.

He tentatively picked it up and perused the pages. The blood drained from his face, eyes widening in shock, at the contents of this black and white decree.

"Mama left this house to you!! How? Why? She told me that she was leaving it as a family house, not just to one of us, as it will bring division!!" He looked at his sister, affirming his previous convictions of their hypocrisy.

"How did you manage to convince Mama to do such a crazy thing?" he continued, beads of perspiration breaking out on his furrowed brows. He felt sick, nauseated. He knew his sister had a mean, wicked streak, never liking him since his birth. She had done cruel things to him throughout their childhood; dropping him to the floor as a baby, at the sight of an oncoming rattle snake, thankfully the poisonous reptile slithered around him, unharmed. When he was 8 years old, she spun him, fast and furious on the playground merry-go-round, becoming dizzy and falling off, with serious injuries to his forehead, barely missing his right eye being gorged out. She got the sweetest "cut tail" from mama for such atrocities!! These were just a couple of the many altercations between them throughout their earlier years! And now this, manipulating their mother in her weakened and vulnerable state.

My God!! When will reprieve come?

Ignoring his question, showing not a single bit of remorse, she continued maliciously, "I know you must go to work tomorrow, but when you return you have one month, to be out of here. Then and only then, will I sign over your assets back to you!"

Jonah could have died in that very moment, welcoming its grip. The betrayals of the women in his life burgeoned further as it dawned on him that his sister had been plotting this all along. She somehow manipulated their mother into granting her the title to their childhood home. The house built with the sweat and blood of their parents, where his umbilical cord was buried in the backyard, now in the possession of his avaricious sister and her partner in crime, husband. He wasn't too concerned about himself, but their brother, Roland who amongst the three of them, were genuinely struggling to survive, as financial hardships trailed his life.

After such a painful divorce, the death of his precious mother and the breakup with Sherry, this was just too much!!

It dawned on him why she had missed church that day before their mother's death- to forcefully coerce their mother to sign over the property to her. The "good' and "stable" one. After all, Roland was a drunken wanderer, who probably would have sold the house for nothing; and Jonah.... well.... he always had a woman to outsmart him out of money and properties.

He laughed hysterically!!

She probably got one of her crooked lawyers to draft up the documents. This was just so wrong!! They were pastors!! Supposed to be leading people...hah!!

More like leading people astray. He thought bitterly.

"Roland and I will fight you on this," he frantically began to get his wits together. "This is unfair, and you know it! You already have so many properties rented out, why must this be another one of your acquisitions? You're just greedy!! Selfish! Bloody hypocrites, both of you!" He growled, rage boiling his blood!

Kenny interjected at this point, before his wife could respond. "We will not advise that, as we WILL make the legal process a lengthy one, and KEEP all your money. And the car, we will report it stolen, as your sister is its legal owner!" He advised.

Jonah was blown away! This was a nightmare, and one that he needed to be awakened from immediately!

After their departure, he called Roland, relating the shocking turn of events. His brother wisely advised Jonah to refrain from legally pursuing the matter in court, as they were hell-bent on claiming ownership. If he retaliated, he could kiss all of his money goodbye. Roland added for good measure, "You see why I can never follow these so called 'Christians,' look what these "pastors" are doing. Just a bunch of hypocrites serving the devil!" "I don't want no part of Christianity!! He exclaimed.

Jonah's back was against the wall. He had no other choice but to vacate his childhood home, maybe never set foot back on its premises again.

Jonah postponed his trip to Russia, citing a family emergency as he sought a suitable apartment for rental. He was disgusted by it all and wanted to be out of that house as soon as possible!

Temptation set in at every side, as the once-dormant demonic voices resurfaced.

Burn the house down to the ground!

Buy a gun and shoot the whole lot of them!

*Stab that b***h sister of yours, and pull her heart out and stomp on it!*

Jonah, pulled himself together, ignoring the evil voices.

They were not worth it. He wanted peace, he just wanted to live a normal life. He moved in to a humble, furnished studio apartment about an hour away. His sister gave him back all his assets, keeping $8,000.00 TT ($1,140.00US) for her troubles.

What a greedy, wicked witch.

Time to move on.

Everyone had their own reward to receive.

God will be the great JUDGE over every heart.

CHAPTER THIRTY-FOUR
WHEN THE TIME IS RIGHT

Isaiah 60:22

When the time is right, I,
THE LORD, will make it happen.

Jonah, returned to his work schedule in 6-week intervals, also rejoining church fellowship and Bible study, with a firm determination to set his life on the right path. His colleagues, however, often made jests at his expense, suggesting that he should forget about women and consider turning to men instead, insinuating that he might have better luck in love with the same gender. These comments left Jonah feeling humiliated and hurt, unable to find any humor in their foolish remarks.

Life for Jonah, steadily became 'normal' again as he dedicated himself to the Lord, putting his desires of the flesh on the back burner once more and seeking God in Spirit and in Truth.

Jonah's heart, however, remained immoveable and implacable. He may find another woman for companionship or even marriage, but he would never love, nor be foolish, like he did before.

On the insistence of one of his co-workers, Jonah downloaded the latest craze in internet circles, **TAGGED,** a social discovery site for playing games, and connecting with like-minded individuals. Similar to FACEBOOK.

He began adding "Friends" and connected with Beverly, a sophisticated and alluring woman. The question lingered: should he pursue this connection? Jonah felt burnt-out relationship-wise and didn't want to rush ahead of God's plan. He believed that his next relationship must be sent by his Father. What he truly sought was a God-fearing, anointed woman like his mother, who knew how to bruise her knees, instead of dirtying her hands in manipulation. After dealing with what felt like endless encounters with deceitful women, Jonah was truly exhausted by the 'Jezebels' he had encountered.

He was offshore, in Russia, when he received the news of Sherry's horrific accident. She was in a taxi cab, from San Fernando to her hometown, where, in order to avoid a head-on collision by an oncoming truck, the driver swerved and crashed into the nearby river.

She was the last to be pulled out of its murky depths.

Jonah, immediately recalled his ex-wife's threat to Sherry... "You would die a horrible death, for destroying my marriage", after they had learnt of another visit to her 'spiritual' church.

Jonah was devastated, rushing to her side upon his return to Trinidad, so thankful that her life was spared. However, the time, spent under contaminated water, had caused permanent damage to her kidney and she now had to be on medication for the rest of her life.

Devastated by her near-death experience, Sherry was thankful to be alive and rededicated her life to the Lord.

Two months later, she was discharged from the hospital and celebrated her renewed life with a thanksgiving ceremony, which Jonah was present to observe. Sherry was deeply grateful for this second chance, coming face to face with the frailty of life and intending to be fully committed to God!

Jonah, too was glad that they were both forgiven of their trespasses, and wanted to move forward. He had surrendered his life solely to God, trusting that all other things will be added, in God's perfect timing!

As for Beverly, she turned out to be a worldly and sophisticated woman, prompting Jonah to step back before getting too involved. Another place in time, she would be a dream come true, her petite, pert figure reveling that she was a gym rat, with such a beautiful face and "dougla" hair.

Nope!

She enjoyed partying, drinking and indulging in Carnival festivities; presenting a form of godliness, by attending religious Mass once a week, but denying the true power of God by her contrary lifestyle!! The antithesis of the woman his mother had been praying for.

Soon after, Jonah stumbled upon another friend suggestion on TAGGED.

Sharon Johnson.

Her profile picture was a pencil sketched photo of 'Jesus' or rather a perception of the Savior, with bible verses, biblical advice and movie quizzes filling her wall. Interestingly her marital status was listed as 'complicated.'

What did that even mean?

Jonah was intrigued.

He sent her a friend request.

A day later, when he got off from work, he saw that she had accepted it. In scrolling through her timeline, it appeared she had children....

"Lord, another one," he rolled his eyes. But, apparently no husband.

Father, this is not the one. This will be Bernice all over again, nope, not happening! Plus, she probably was so hideous, as she had no pictures of herself; only those of her children. They were some good-looking children, though!

In their subsequent exchanges about Bible verses and scriptures, he felt that she was unusual, not asking about his work, even though he had posted photos of him from his travel all over the world, so that at a glance, it will tell the tale of his adventurous globetrotting. He did not put his address as Trinidad, but instead Louisiana, U.S.A.

She still failed to ask him anything about his work, job or voyages. That was very unusual for him, as women flock to him once they realize his status in life.

Hmmmmm.

The topic was always God-centered.

He told her that he was visiting Trinidad soon, and maybe they could eventually meet up. She appeared nervous by its prospect, hesitating when he asked for her number.

"I don't give my numbers to strangers" was her curt response.

Okay, that was a first. The first female to not eagerly give him their number. Maybe she might be the one after all! He felt a thrill he had not felt in such a very long time. He had not even met this girl, not even seen what she looked like, but he was giddy with excitement on meeting her.

This was definitely a first for him!!

He compromised. He typed;

OK... let me give you my number, so you can contact me instead. Will you be comfortable with that?

She agreed.

He was scheduled to return home in about three weeks. However, due to a work deadline, he ended up overstaying by a full six weeks in Russia, having now spent 12 weeks there. He yearned for home and the excitement of meeting Ms. Sharon Johnson.

They were extremely strapped for workers, and needed all hands-on deck, so he was only going home for 8 days!!

Arriving in Trinidad late on a Friday night, Jonah figured Sharon would not call as it was almost midnight. But he anticipated her call the next day, Saturday, barely sleeping due to thoughts of her, even though he was severely jet lagged.

What did she look like?

What would her voice sound like?

When Saturday passed without a call, he spent the balance of the weekend in turmoil. He wondered if she had set him up, as he had reminded her before leaving that he was definitely coming in, so he was expecting her to get in touch with him.

By Monday, he was anxious and frustrated. Finally, in the wee hours of the morning, he received a message on TAGGED from her. She explained she had tried calling multiple times but got a recording indicating that his number was out of service.

"I guess it's not meant for us to meet," she summarized!

Jonah's heart pounded in his chest.

He responded immediately!

What number did I give to you?

He had indeed given her the wrong number – it was off by one figure.

He corrected it and requested she call him immediately.

He could kick himself for the torture he had put himself through over the weekend. He only had 8 days and this was already the third day.... time was racing, and he had yet to hear her voice or meet her.

She complied.

When Sharon called, her voice sounded angelic, well spoken, with very little broken English that was synonymous with the "Trini" twang. She was truly different, as chilling goose bumps surged through his body, with every word she spoke.

Can he fall in love with someone's voice and charisma over the phone? Without even knowing what she looked like?

She made him feel COMFORTABLE for want of a better word.

At rest!

At peace!

Like he was finally home!

This has got to be my future wife. My true wife.

Rib of my rib and bone of my bone, a prayer his mother had uttered on his behalf almost all of her life!

CHAPTER THIRTY-FIVE
HE WHO FINDS A WIFE

Proverbs 18:22NIV)

He who finds a wife, find what is good and receives favor from the LORD

They agreed to meet at a popular mall in the Central area. She opted for a public place, for personal safety.

Sharon had never done anything like this before.

Sitting there, awaiting his arrival, Sharon felt a mix of conflicting emotions and thoughts. Maybe this wasn't a good idea after all. This wasn't what she had envisioned when she accepted his friend request. The idea of meeting someone she had connected with online seemed surreal; after all he lived in Louisiana. Moreover, she had many friends on the app, but never anticipated actually meeting any of them. She definitely wasn't looking for a relationship. Having been a 'wife' for many years to someone who had used and abused her in lascivious sexual activities, while failing miserably in his roles as a husband and a father, made her wary.

Her father, Edmund Matthews, her pillar of strength, had passed away the year before, and she was still in mourning, clad in solemn black attire. It seemed like those colors might be her permanent wardrobe now.

For most of their married life, they lived with her dad in a house owned jointly by her father and his sister, her aunt Catherine. They previously lived with the children's paternal grandparents, but after the birth of her second child, they were no longer welcomed in their house, seen as a burden rather than a blessing, and were asked to leave.... not in the kindest of ways. Thankfully, her father graciously offered them refuge, had he not done so, would have probably rendered them homeless. Life had been incredibly tough. Although they didn't pay rent, Sharon struggled to hold down three jobs to meet the growing demands of her family. She always felt like a single parent, her children's father seemingly unable to hold down a proper job; impervious and uncaring to the needs of his family. Verbal and physical abuse, financial constraints, and poverty were all they had ever known. It was a "hard knock life."

After her dad's death, her aunt wasted no time in issuing eviction notices. The situation was now in the court's hands, as her father had wanted her and his grandchildren to continue living there. It was his dying wish!

Sharon shuddered as she reflected on her past. She attended a Catholic convent and in her quest for God; keenly aware that she was called from her mother's womb; was seriously considering becoming a nun. Instead, she had been pushed into marriage at the tender age of 17, her mother forcing her to work at 15 and taking all her earnings. It felt like a form of modern-day slavery. She was deprived of pursuing further academical studies. In the midst of her inner turmoil, she met this 26-year-old man who made promises of taking care of her. He offered her a place to stay, at his mother's house, where she would at least have food to eat, something that was lacking in her home. Desperate for an escape from the bondage of her childhood, Sharon reluctantly accepted. It was like a choice between this marriage and an unthinkable alternative – suicide.

He portrayed himself as a 'Christian' man; Sharon, having given her life to the Lord just the year before. A babe in Christ.

However, it turned out to be a façade. He was actually a Hindu posing as a Christian just to get closer to her. He admitted that from the moment he laid eyes on her, he desired her sexually. This revelation left her feeling degraded and regretful, especially since she found out she was pregnant. At just 18 years old, she had no idea how to navigate being a wife and a soon-to-mother.

Their marriage grew more complicated over the years. Four children later, Sharon was still working tirelessly to provide for them, while her husband showed little to no regard for his responsibilities. They eventually separated when she caught him cheating with young teenage girls online. He was also found collecting nude photos of other women on pornographic sites.

Previously, he was offered an opportunity to work in Canada, through a government-funded project, known colloquially as "picking apples." However, instead of using this opening for a fresh start, to provide for his family, he immersed himself in the enticing but destructive lifestyle of the country. He frequented the alluring lights of strip clubs weekly, reveling in the company of loose women. Tragically, one of these encounters led to him bringing back a disease that nearly claimed Sharon's life. It was a harrowing experience that left her fighting for survival, a stark reminder of the depths of his betrayal and recklessness.

Through it all, Sharon felt she had made a mockery of God and the sacrament of marriage.

Thank God for the cleansing blood!!

In the midst of their divorce proceedings Sharon found herself at a crossroads. The idea of diving into another relationship was the furthest thing from her mind; all she desired was to forge ahead as a single mother, focusing on her children. Love, in the romantic sense, had always seemed like an elusive dream to her, an illusion, as the Mills and Boon novels, that engrossed her early teenaged years, it was a concept she could barely grasp. The only love she truly felt and understood was the deep affection she had for her deceased father, her three sons and daughter.

The scars of her past, including the sexual torment from her half-brother and the betrayal of her soon-to-be ex-husband, had left her emotionally battered. As the divorce drew nearer, doubts crept in, and she began to question the decisions she had made. Yet, she couldn't deny the spark of curiosity and apprehension that fluttered within her as she thought of Jonah. She had never shared any photos of herself, yet she had seen images of him. His handsome features filled her thoughts, stirring emotions she never knew existed, until now.

The prospect of meeting him face to face both excited and terrified her. Questions swirled in her mind as she sat waiting in the crowded mall.

"This is a horrible idea" she bemoaned, inwardly crushing the anxiety taking over her mind.

Sharon froze, as she spotted him, just as she made the move to get up out of her seat. She saw him frantically searching the bustling mall. If he doesn't figure out who she is, she will never reveal herself to him, taking it as a sign to let it be....

Meanwhile, Jonah's searched continued, frustration mounting with each passing moment. It seemed ludicrous to him that Sharon, the woman he connected with online, was so reluctant to share photos or even her phone number. Despite his growing impatience, he couldn't deny the sense of anticipation building within him, a surge of adrenalin coursing through his veins, at the thought of finally meeting this mysterious woman. He scanned the crowd, with a sense of excitement and nervousness, and couldn't shake the feeling that this encounter could be the start of something extraordinary.

His gaze locked onto her, as she sat looking straight at him.

HER!!!

It was her.

The "sweet looking reds" he had glimpsed in the room next to his mother on that sad day she had passed, the angelic woman deep in prayer for an elderly gentleman.

Was this truly Sharon? His heart raced as he made his way towards her, a mix of emotions swirling within him.

Jonah couldn't shake the memories flooding back- the heartache from Paula's betrayal threatening to overwhelm him. He had made a promise to himself years ago, a promise that echoed in his mind as he approached her. In Trinidad, there's a saying:

'The only good red thing is a TT one dollar bill."

He couldn't help but wonder if this encounter was destined to bring more heartache or an answer to prayer.

As he drew closer, their eyes continued to be mutually fixated on each other, time seeming to stand still. Sharon's breath caught in her throat, her heart racing with uncertainty. When Jonah finally stood in front of her, she struggled to catch her breath, her eyes wide with surprise and anticipation.

How did he figure it out?

"Sharon?" he asked, his voice tinged with uncertainty, unsure if he truly wanted it to be her.

"Yes, hello", she replied, a sparkling smile lighting up her eyes and face. Jonah felt a sinking sensation in the pit of his stomach. This encounter could break him, and he knew it. The rapturous intensity of his emotions was overwhelming, something entirely new and unfamiliar.

My wife....

But this is not who he wanted her to be.

Not even sure what he was expecting 'her' to be!

CHAPTER THIRTY-SIX
The heart of stone

Ezekiel 36:26

I will give you a new heart and put a new spirit within you; and I will take the heart of stone out of your flesh and give you a heart of flesh

The electricity between them was palpable as he leaned down to peck her on the cheek, his heart pounding in his chest. He felt like a teenager again, dumbstruck by the captivating presence of this woman before him. She was undeniably pretty, but it was more than that.

Her aura.... Something that drew him in like a moth to a flame.

"I know you" he admitted, his voice barely above a whisper.

"How do you know me?" she laughed nervously, her eyes shining with conflicting emotions. She was certain that he was going to come up with the lame "pick up" line that he saw her "in his dreams!!"

When Jonah revealed to her where exactly, a wave of sadness latched onto her gorgeous face. He noticed immediately the moisture in her eyes. She wore very little makeup, her skin unblemished and radiant. It was a stark contrast to the women from his past, who often wore layers of makeup to hide their flaws. Sharon's skin was like porcelain, evoking emotions in him that he had never experienced before.

Tears welled in her eyes as she explained that her father had passed away that very day, and she had been praying for a peaceful transition for him. Jonah couldn't believe his ears - they had both lost their parents on that same fateful day, a day that seemed to blur the lines between life and death.

In that moment, as they sat facing each other, it felt as though their paths had unknowingly crossed, as if it was meant to be. Jonah couldn't shake the feeling that this was the elusive woman his mother had prayed for him to find, the woman who would change his life in ways he could never have imagined.

They exchanged brief histories of their lives, at first hesitant to reveal too much, but soon found themselves talking for hours, completely lost in each other's company. Time slipped away as they shared their stories, unaware of the world around them.

Just then, her phone rang, - it was her sister Denise. She told no one of her adventurous trip to the mall, Denise was babysitting her children and was concerned as the time had passed where she was due to return. School was closed for the Easter vacation, so it was stressful, having always to find someone to watch them. Especially when she had to work. Thankfully, recently she mostly worked from home so was extremely thankful for God's tender mercies.

As Sharon got up to leave, Jonah's heart somersaulted. He didn't want them to part ways. He could look at her always and forever. He felt the urge to talk to her, to pour his heart out to her.

She mesmerized him with her intellect....

And something else....it felt like Angels were around her, watching her, favoring her.

Guarding her.

He never experienced anything like this!

NEVER!!

With a sheepish grin, she finally gave him her number, relating the confidence to do so, as she felt comfortable with him, now that he had proven he wasn't a serial killer!

He laughed heartily.

The sound echoing throughout the emptying mall.

A profound joy, unlike anything he had ever experienced, radiated through his mind, body and soul. The connection he felt with this woman was undeniable, and he was certain that she felt it too as they locked eyes and souls, reluctantly parting ways in sweet sorrow.

Jonah was exhilarated.

Happy.

Joyous.

Jonah walked away from the mall that evening, with a sense of elation he hadn't felt in years. At last, it seemed that his mother's prayers had been answered. He had met that 'special' woman she had prayed for him to find.

Despite the happiness that filled his heart, doubts lingered in the back of his mind. Could this be real? Was Sharon too good to be true? He steeled himself against the possibility of heartbreak, reminding himself to take things slow and not let his emotions run away with him.

They embarked on a year and a half of courtship, savoring each moment before finally exchanging vows on the breathtaking shores of his hometown Mayaro. The ceremony, officiated by his mother's pastor, was a blend of serene beauty and solemnity. In a separate celebration, they honored the memories of both their deceased parents, who had departed from this world on the same day. It was a poignant moment, marking the transition from life to death for their parents and from death to life for Jonah and Sharon's shared journey.

Jonah felt such peace in his soul.

Surely life from now on could be nothing short of bliss with this remarkable woman by his side.

He eagerly anticipated the prospect of having many babies together, especially with Sharon still within childbearing age.

Yet, despite these hopeful thoughts, dark clouds of doubt and suspicion blanketed his mind, causing a series of bleak notions, and 'what if's.'

Their honeymoon was brief, as Jonah was scheduled to fly back to Russia for a special assignment. However, what he experienced with Sharon was a purity of connection that he had never felt before. Their souls literally merged and fused at the consummation of their union. It was all so surreal, and an experience that was never duplicated.

Life will be wonderful....

Jonah, however, had a double mind, that still doubted this reality. She was too good to be true. No woman could be this "perfect;" mentally preparing himself for potential challenges, with a backlash or two.

His heart, hardened and stony by past traumas, refused to relinquish his total self into this marriage.

"WE can easily forgive a child who is afraid of the dark; the real tragedy of life is when men are afraid of the light."

Plato

CHAPTER THIRTY-SEVEN
A companion of fools

Proverbs 13:20

He who walks with wise men will be wise, but the companion of fools will be destroyed.

"By all means, marry; you will be happy if you get a good wife. If you get a bad one, you will become a philosopher."

Socrates

Jonah's work situation soon shifted when he was stationed in the U.S.A., to a more suitable rotation for a newlywed. His bosses decided on a month-on and month-off schedule, wanting him to spend quality time with his new wife, Sharon.

Both Jonah and Sharon were elated at this change.

Despite the distance, Jonah kept in constant communication with his bride. Fear and anxiety sometimes crept in, especially if Sharon failed to answer his calls immediately. They Skyped whenever possible; Jonah eager to keep track of her whereabouts. Although he hadn't put her name on anything official, he made sure she had what she needed while he was away. Sharon, being a working woman; unlike his two previous wives; didn't rely on his money. She had a rent-free home, and a stock of at least two months' supply of groceries, bought before his departure. Jonah meticulously managed everything, intent on not repeating past mistakes.

Before their marriage, Sherry made several attempts to contact Jonah. Each time Jonah declined her calls, a little bit perturbed by her relentless pursuit of their relationship.

His brother Roland, instantly disliked Sharon, insisting she was 'a gold digger.' He even boldly declared this to Sharon's friend and chief bridesmaid, Pamela. His sister, Cindy, viewed Sharon as another in Jonah's long string of conquests, and had washed her hands off of him, arrogantly stating, that if Sharon betrayed him like the others, he shouldn't come crawling to her and her husband for help. As if he would ever solicit her help again, given what she and her husband had done!

Despite just celebrating their first anniversary, Jonah and Sharon were already facing challenges. Jonah felt overwhelmed by all the negative talk about his wife from his family. They accused Sharon of playing a manipulative game to get his money, which couldn't have been further from the truth.

Sharon had already suffered two miscarriages, the last one was almost fatal, being ectopic, which caused her to be hospitalized overnight. All these incidents happened while Jonah was 'away' at work, raising 'red flags' in his mind.

Pamela, Sharon's friend, had accepted a job to Mexico. Jonah befriending her on TAGGED and began communicating with her on Skype, perhaps as a backup plan in case things went downhill with Sharon. As much as he loved her, and knew both their souls were inadvertently, interwoven and intertwined with an inexplicable yearning for her, Jonah was burnt beyond salvaging, his heart black and empty.

Sherry kept haunting Jonah's thoughts. A stronghold that was difficult to release. Her calls persisted. So were her texting, especially on his birthday, Christmas and their "anniversary" of consummating their illicit affair. Jonah couldn't understand why she was insistent on reconnecting. She was the one who grew distant and cold, abruptly ending their relationship a couple of months after his divorce to Bernice. Then after the near-death experience, which changed her perspective of life, gave herself back to Jesus. So, what was her motivation now?

Jonah, overly confident in his charm and charisma, was not prepared for Pamela to rattle to Sharon, of his unwanted advances to her, with his persistent calls on Skype, and the absurd advice of "please don't tell Sharon, that we speak!" Trouble began brewing between Jonah and Sharon, from that day forward. Sharon's suspicion of her husband grew; and Jonah became more deceitful in his dealings with her! He lied constantly to her, covering up a lie with a lie.

One day, upon seeing another text from Sherry, Jonah foolishly decided to respond. This decision proved fatal for Jonah, opening a door to calamity and chaos in his life. Sherry, obsessed with Jonah, led him down a dangerous path with her seductive words, akin to the warnings in **Proverbs 7**.

Jonah learned that Sherry was having serious marital problems as her husband Gregory had returned to alcohol, causing her shame in her community. She revealed to Jonah that he was always her true love, and would always love him. Just the words needed from the lips of 'Satan' for Jonah to fall back into his philandering ways.

Jonah sought constant validation, always seeking solace from outside sources, namely women, instead of the Source of Life only found in Jesus Christ. Sharon besieged him with nagging accusations of cheating, even getting revelations in her dreams that were tormenting her at nights.

Sharon's sister, Denise, whom they both employed as a humanitarian gesture, whispered to Jonah, to not be beguiled by her sweet and innocent behavior. Hinting that Sharon, in his absence, still had an ongoing relationship with her ex.

This painful revelation set fireworks off in Jonah's mind.... Becoming the nail in the coffin for him, confirming his fears that Sharon was like his previous wives and lovers.

Apparently the only good woman was a dead one! Sherry was a drug that he couldn't get out of his system, she offered him what no other woman did. She just wanted to have a "good time" with him, with no strings attached. He appreciated her for her "honesty"! She had no qualms in being the side chick....and Jonah had no problem with that. He felt macho; having a wife and "a deputy". This type of lifestyle was applauded in Trinidad....and worldwide.

Jonah was heading to Thailand for a project that will last four to six years. Jonah was thrilled, as he had never ventured to that part of the world; and the prospect of plundering new territory excited him.

Sharon was not as enthusiastic. He would be gone for six weeks, only returning home for a mere ten days. This was a stark contrast to his month-on, month-off rotation they had enjoyed since their marriage began. They were already having serious marital issues. Despite the deep love and connection, he felt with her, Jonah decided that perhaps this time away would do them good.

Meanwhile, Sharon began praying earnestly for their tumultuous marriage. She had never loved anyone like she loved Jonah; there was something about him that lured her soul.

She had previously read somewhere, **"You never know how broken someone is until you try to love them..."** This truth became a reality in her relationship with Jonah, the more she tried to love him, the more elusive he became!

She continued in prayer for her husband.

Jonah, on the other side of the mountain, began experiencing guilt of his ongoing tete-a-tete with Sherry. To make amends, he decided to surprise Sharon with a trip to St Lucia as a belated anniversary gift. He had noticed that she really did appear to genuinely love him, relating to him that she was constantly praying for him.

No other woman ever offered that sacrifice of incense to God's throne ROOM on his behalf. She also made a big deal in celebrating his birthday, surprising him many a time, constantly showering him with expensive gifts! From her own hard-earned money, not financed by him for himself!!

No one ever, not even his previous "wives" had the heart to celebrate any of these occasions, only his mother... and even then, it was very limited due to her impoverished state.

Jonah realized that perhaps those who doubted Sharon were wrong. Her fruits were godly, and not rotten as they all had implied, having all virtues and temperament of the Proverbial 31 woman... they were all simply envious and jealous, not wanting him to finally be happy and contented in his marriage. Doubts plagued his mind yet again, torn between breaking it off with Sherry and being totally committed to Sharon.

All hell broke loose during their romantic vacation in St Lucia, when Sharon discovered

Jonah's indiscretion with Sherry. Panicking, Jonah lied his way out of the situation, suddenly fearful of losing his wife, and truly wanting his marriage to work. As soon as he landed back in Trinidad, he cut off all contact with Sherry, blocking and deleting her numbers from his phone. Sherry was devastated.

Jonah reiterated his commitment to Sharon, in making their marriage work as he recommitted his life to the Lord, and his precious wife.

However, Sharon soon realized that Jonah may love her desperately with his feelings but still not know how to love her correctly through his actions!

Jonah truly wanted his marriage to work, and the wake-up call in St. Lucia was a turning point for him. Sharon hoped that this would mark a new beginning for their relationship, a chance for Jonah to learn how to truly love and trust her and be fully committed to their life together.

CHAPTER THIRTY-EIGHT
DARKENED IN THEIR UNDERSTANDING

Ephesians 4:18 NIV

They are darkened in their understanding and separated from the life of GOD because of the ignorance that is in them due to the hardening of their hearts.

Life seemed blissful, at least from Sharon's perspective. After the chaos in St. Lucia, Jonah transformed into the epitome of a loving and devoted husband. They even started considering IVF as an option after multiple unsuccessful attempts of conception.

Sharon had long discontinued her TAGGED account; but Jonah did not follow suit. Throughout their marriage, he continued pursuing other women, and his attempt at fidelity was short-lived. Unknown to Sharon, Jonah had a history of women in every country he worked in before meeting her, and Thailand was no exception. The allure of Thai women, with their sensuality. beckoned Jonah's wandering eyes and lustful desires. They were plentiful, each one eager to please the "farangs," being drawn like moths to a flame to his accent and good looks.

Soon, Jonah befriended Malai, a young and beautiful woman from Bangkok, who from inception insisted on maintaining a monogamous relationship. To prove his love and commitment, they got married in a civil ceremony, despite Malai's insistence on having a Buddhist temple wedding, Jonah adamantly rejected such a sacrilegious suggestion.

Upon Jonah's return home, he played the perfect husband to Sharon, shunning any hint of guilt he may have felt. Their two failed attempts at IVF procedures threatened to drain his finances, making him less inclined to go through that again. Additionally, Malai offered the prospect of bearing him a child, which further justified Jonah's duplicity in his mind. He honestly had no idea how this was going to play out but his desperation for a child threw caution to the wind.

During the night, Jonah would awaken to speak for hours to Malai, as it was daytime over in Thailand. He would hide his phone, keeping it under his pillow, a behavior Sharon found odd but chose to remain silent about. Her dreams intensified, haunted by the specter of Jonah's infidelity.

She remembered his behavior years ago when she brought up the subject; she no longer had the fight or fortitude to go through that experience again. His tongue was a dangerous weapon to her fragile heart.

Five years passed with many false alarms of pregnancy, with his 'wife' Malai, leaving Jonah disheartened. Eventually, he 'annulled' his marriage to her, finding her no longer appealing or useful. With the Thailand project coming to an end, Jonah saw fit to block and delete Malai's number, erasing her from his life.

Sharon was unaware of this clandestine affair; Jonah believed it was crucial to keep it that way. He feared Sharon's reaction, knowing she might promptly divorce him and take his assets just like his previous wives.

Soon, Jonah was to embark on another work assignment in a different country. Malai would become a distant memory, another conquest in his long line of women. Jonah felt a sense of machismo, convinced he had bedded more women than his peers.

However, Jonah's unfaithful acts were soon to be exposed by a force beyond his control. The whole situation exploded far worse than the St. Lucia fiasco, leaving Jonah genuinely ashamed and devastated at the pain he caused Sharon……again.

Sharon was shattered, seemingly beyond repair. Despite Jonah's earlier commitment after she found out about Sherry, this scandal with Malai blew up as the s*** hit the fan, scattering filthy excrements over their already fragile marriage. As Jonah pleaded for forgiveness, Sharon did not believe it's genuineness, retorting he was only sorry because he got caught….

After several attempts at marriage counselling and ardent fellowshipping at their local church; things eventually settled after many months.

By this time Sharon had changed. She became bitter and suspicious, constantly obsessing over Jonah's every move. Jonah felt trapped, regretting the choices that led to this situation.

"She was only a wife" he thought arrogantly. "She didn't birth him!"

She was not around in his earlier life where his mother fought tooth and nail, just to keep him alive.

She was replaceable!

The excessive tongue-lashing exuding from her mouth, her incessant berating, was getting to him, as the voices in his head sought relief from her tempestuous verbiage!

Jonah received an email from Sherry. This woman was indeed persistent! No matter how many times they broke off their relationship, something (or someone) always pulled them back together. He found himself drawn back into that web of deceit once more.

Seeking reprieve from Sharon's constant nagging, they rekindled their affair. Sharon grew more agitated as she knew that he was being unfaithful again, causing further disrepair and disrepute to their already frazzled marriage.

The outbreak of Covid-19 further strained their relationship. Jonah's inability to work for more than a year due to the pandemic devastated his finances. He resented Sharon's constant nagging. He wished she would disappear sometimes, as the intense love he had once for her were diminishing by the day.

He began feeling that love for Sherry.

She was the only constant in his life. Always there for him at the most crucial times of his life, and most importantly, never nags him!!

Expressing his feelings to Sherry, they plotted together on how to get rid of Sharon, in a diplomatic way.... after all, it would be illegal for him to throw her out of their marital home, the house was bought at the beginning of their marriage and she already lived there for 10 years. However, he can trick her out, take away her keys, change all the locks, and bar her entry to the home!

He could take her name off all the utility bills, thereby having no claim, to anything! It was the perfect plan, and one that Sherry would ensure was executed. She was getting older, and those other men in her life, was nothing like Jonah.

He was kind and sweet to her, as she had intended. And he had money!! A great job, and his own home! Maybe this time she would marry him, though the prospect held no appeal to her before, as he was not the only fish in her pond back then, and her children were small; she was finally ready to become the illustrious Mrs. Jonah Foster.

They succeeded in their devious plan, leaving Sharon devastated and homeless. She begged and pleaded to Jonah for good sense to prevail at this madness that was inflicted upon their life, which made no sense whatsoever to her!

Jonah, was totally captivated with Sherry, his "new" and exhilarating 'wife'. This was who he was supposed to be with, all along. Totally obliterating his wife Sharon, as an outcast, his one wish was for her to leave him alone and move on with her life. She would not spare words in pointing out to him that their marriage was a sham, and he was an unfaithful, useless bastard. So let her move on as he had already done, quite content to live the rest of his days with Sherry.

Their 11th anniversary came, with Jonah calling the police on her. She had gone to the house, learning that Sherry was now officially living in her home with her husband!! She made an uproar and a huge scene with the police threatening to taser her as they unceremoniously forced her out the gate.

Devastation was an understatement to how she felt. She longed to be awakened from this nightmare, as those dreams, she had in times past was now her reality!!

Two weeks later, Sharon drove down to their home around 7pm, in a last-ditch effort to talk sense into her husband. She called him, before venturing there, as she said she needed to urgently speak to him. She had already made a fool of herself two weeks earlier and just wanted to have a civil conversation with her husband.

Gregory, Sherry's husband had been in constant communication with her, revealing things about his wife, Sherry that Jonah needed to know. Gregory revealed to Sharon that his wife and Jonah had an on-and-off again affair for many years and it was like an obsession on both their parts. He also indicated to Sharon, that Sherry can no longer bear children, as she had a hysterectomy many years ago! Further to that, Sherry had multiple affair partners, mostly married men, as her insatiable desire for gold and money fueled her reckless, wanton lifestyle. Gregory was totally fed-up and wanted to divorce this permissive woman who only brought dishonor and shame to their marriage from its inception.

Jonah needed to hear about the antics of his precious 'wife.'

Jonah came out and began chastising her. Accusing her of atrocities that were far from the truth. Who could be feeding him such lies?

Sharon proceeded to explain all that she had learnt from Gregory, but Jonah refused to listen to anything she had to say!

He rudely informed her that she was no longer his wife, as Sherry was his new 'wife' and she needed to accept that and move on with a new man.

Sharon interjected that Sherry can never love him the way she did. Jonah became livid in anger. He retorted that Sherry will be there for him through, thick and thin, and if anything were to happen to him, she will be the one to care for him.

"Gregory seems to be infatuated with you, go with him!" he spat out!

Sharon was devastated.

Rain began falling at that point and Sharon had nowhere in which to shelter. Jonah ran inside the house, not before coldly instructing her to leave. They had nothing further to discuss, and to never set foot again on his premises.

Sharon just stood there immobilized in shock. Oblivious to the rain drops that soaked through her numb and battered soul! Jonah was exasperated and just wanted her dead at this point!! He hated her very being, her voice and everything about her!!

Meanwhile, Sherry was upset that Sharon had come by, promising to up her "GAME", determined to solidify her position as the new 'wife". That woman must never set foot again in her house! This was her house now, and Jonah belonged to her. She vowed to ensure that Jonah divorced Sharon and cut off all communication between Sharon and Gregory, as he had been revealing damning information about Jonah and Sherry's affair, as well as her past indiscretions!!

He is talking too much!!

Jonah must believe that I am the woman that he had always loved and wanted! Nothing and no one must come between us.... ever again!!

True to her intention, Gregory suddenly blocked Sharon, not before berating her for going to Jonah with all the juicy dirt, he had given to her about his wife, Sherry!

"You're a trouble maker!" He yelled at her before slamming the phone down in her ear.

That was an absolute turn around, as Gregory was the one who reached out to her, even revealing his willingness to go to court on her behalf to fight Jonah for everything!

Witchcraft was certainly a **PREDOMINANT** factor at play in this dangerous game!

Sharon, relentlessly, continued to **pray and fast** for her husband.

CHAPTER THIRTY-NINE
THE PRESENCE OF GOD

Psalm 68:2

As smoke is driven away, so drive them away; as wax melteth before the fire, so let the wicked perish at the presence of GOD

Jonah and Sherry were finally living together in Sharon's matrimonial home as 'husband and wife.' Sherry was ecstatic, feeling like the happiest woman in the world. She had Jonah exactly where she wanted him, deeply in love with her and resenting his 'former' wife Sharon.

Jonah's former declarations of Sharon being his 'soulmate,' 'his forever and always,' 'his one true love,' and 'a love he'd never known before,' irritated Sherry to the core.

She dealt with that foolish talk; her jealousy unleashed as she considered, that in all the many years that they were together, Jonah had never been this passionate about their love.

Jonah spared no expense in showering Sherry with love and compassion, and they seemed to be living in total bliss. However, not all that glitters is gold...

Around the second year of their cohabiting, Jonah began to feel a stirring in his spirit, an unease and restlessness. He desired peace in his relationship and sought validation that they were on the right path. To further solidify their union, he started introducing Sherry as his new wife to his distant relatives in his hometown of Mayaro, dismissing Sharon as his ex-wife. He dared not go around his best friend "Lovey", because he would have told him, in no uncertain terms, that he was in blatant sin and needed to reconcile with Sharon.

Despite Sherry's hints that it was time for them to officially marry, Jonah staunchly refused. He cited his three failed marriages, declaring "three strikes you're out" and had no intention of divorcing Sharon to marry Sherry. He had enough of this façade called "marriage."

His blatant refusal left Sherry feeling frustrated and desperate.

"We will see about that!" She whispered under her breath.

Upon returning from a four-month job expedition in Thailand, Jonah received a troubling phone call from Sharon. She had just returned from a 6-month hiatus to Texas, with a disturbing revelation from God: that Jonah and Sherry would be involved in a fatal vehicular accident, resulting in her death and his paralysis. Jonah was perturbed and quickly hung up on her, dismissing the prediction as gloomy and unwelcome.

When Jonah shared Sharon's prophecy with Sherry, she waved it off as the ramblings of a desperate and scorned woman.

"Baby, ignore that jacka**," "she's a narcissistic, obsessive witch, who cannot accept the fact that you no longer love nor want her" she assured him.

Jonah was far from feeling 'ASSURED.'

Jonah's restless spirit persisted, and feeling incredibly overwhelmed, made the decision to commence going back to 'the house of the Lord,' much to Sherry's reluctance.

Sherry noticed a change in Jonah; he seemed grouchy and distant as their once passionate relationship became frigid and platonic; she felt more like his sister. Despite her feverish attempts to reignite their passion (through her "brew" and placement of 'substance' in his meals) Jonah still seemed uninterested and preoccupied. She felt powerless and was losing ground!

At times, Jonah had to meet with Sharon to collect money for a legal matter unrelated to their marriage, which always made Sherry uncomfortable. She despised the fact that his ex-wife, as she termed her, was indirectly helping Jonah with these legal fees and she just knew that Sharon was hoping it would endear her more to him.

Sherry secretly wanted to be Sharon. She was an incredibly beautiful woman, with a captivating personality, and Sherry found herself doing the worst of the worst in order for Jonah to eradicate the feelings he truly felt for Sharon.

They both began partaking of holy communion, hoping to appease this upheaval he felt in his spirit, but it grew in intensity.

The situation took a darker turn when the pastor of the church they were attending contacted them, warning that they would face a terrible accident, resulting in their deaths unless they followed God's instructions.

Jonah instantly recalled Sharon's grim warning to him months before, which he had scoffed at, now realizing that this was confirmation. The pastor had no prior knowledge of Sharon, and vice versa. Sherry grew fearful and feebly began rebuking it in Jesus' Name.

In a twist of fate, Jonah started to appreciate Sharon's previous efforts in their marriage. He reflected on how Sharon would never hesitate to help him, unlike Sherry. Memories of Sharon's kindness and graciousness began to haunt him, as he began coming out of the stupor and trance that Sherry had placed upon him many years ago.

Suddenly, Jonah's eyes were becoming opened to the truth. What was he doing with this devourer? This woman would not put forward even 5 cents to help him, in anything, ever!!!

At his last birthday, he had to sponsor himself with dinner, and she had the audacity to invite her girlfriend Maria, and her husband, Wendell to the birthday celebration, in which he had to be the fool to foot the entire bill!!

Sharon may be many things, but she would NOT have done that to him!! Now, here it was that Sharon, who no longer lived, nor was welcomed in his house, helping him with the legal fees in the ensuing court matter with the con artist, who fraudulently took a downpayment from them in 2013, aborting the renovations to be done, breaching the contract they had signed.

He saw the transformation in Sharon. She was no longer perturbed, bitter or angry, the few times they met, she was always gracious and kind to him. He saw a light in her, that was there before, when they had first met, but now had magnified and multiplied in intensity. She was never judgmental. Always loving in her approach and speech.

She recounted at one of their meetups, that she went up to his home town of Mayaro, visiting his mother's grave side, to 'complain' to her!!

She related to him, "I said, Mama, here I am, the woman you were praying for your son to finally meet and marry, and he threw me away!" She laughed.

He looked at her quizzically, doubting her words. She showed him several pictures from her phone gallery as proof.

Jonah was stunned.

She really does love me!

The thought hit him like a ton of bricks. He was broken.

He felt his heart begin to melt at what could only be the presence of God, that wrapped itself around him!! Such a presence that exuded from her and unto him. It was an inexplicable feeling, as he hastily bade her goodbye, masking his turbulent thoughts.

He had to get out of her presence; as rays of blinding light began illuminating his mind.

He felt his eyes literally open as the scales fell away. He felt his ears unstopped, as the realization of what he had done, not just to Sharon, but throughout his life, slapped him in his face.

He saw himself; his reflection was loathsome!

He was playing the fool all of his life, recklessly entangled in the wicked game of debauchery, deceit and degradation.

He felt his tongue burning as coals of purification was placed upon it.

The filter of the Holy Spirit surrounded him, as he drove home that morning.

Jonah wept bitterly!! Years of pent-up tears, now gushed forth with a ferocity that threatened to overwhelm him with guilt and shame. Jonah felt the full brunt of his sins, recognizing the destructive path he had been on. The Holy Spirit continued its relentless pursuit at his heart as the heat of God's love slowly melted the unyielding walls around his stony heart.

The following Sunday, after a week of immense pressure from the Holy Spirit to reconcile with Sharon, Jonah whipped up the courage to text Sharon, via WhatsApp in the wee hours of the morning with 15, vague, subliminal messages of sorrow and regret and his intention to restore their fractured marriage.

He finally "saw" Sherry for what she was in his life; a hideous, monstrous beast in human form, relentless in the pursuit of his ultimate destruction. He began to smell the evil that permeated his atmosphere, repugnant to his nostrils and enlightened spirit.

Jonah yearned for his freedom!

Jonah's mind spiraled out of control, as the psychological warfare between Satan and the Ruach Elohim of God blew fresh wind and cleansing fire over his soul, as it encircled him.

'Consider how precious a soul must be, when both God and the devil are after it."

-Charles Spurgeon-

His inner turmoil was witnessed by Sherry, as she grew fearful that this might be the annihilation and obliteration of their relationship.

Indeed, it was!

What followed in the weeks to come was nothing short of divine intervention in Jonah's and Sharon's lives.

"God does nothing but in answer to prayer; and even they who have been converted to God without praying for it themselves, (which is exceedingly rare,) were not without the prayers of others."

- John Wesley -

For an in-depth exploration of Jonah's and Sharon's marital journey, their trials and the profound story of their restoration and reconciliation, I Invite you to delve into the pages of the book titled, **"STANDING ON S(h)IFTING SAND."** This narrative weaves a compelling tale of their marriage, navigating through their challenges, and ultimately finding a path to healing and renewal.

Accompanying this narrative is a prayer guide that goes hand in hand with their story. Filled with potent prayers and exhortation, these words were inspired and downloaded from the Holy Spirit. The prayer guide is designed to lead readers through their own reflections, prayers, and steps toward faith, restoration and reconciliation. It offers a moving and insightful resource for those seeking guidance and inspiration in their own fight towards marriage restoration.

Both books are available on Amazon.

EPILOGUE

Through the lens of JONAH'S JOURNEY.... A Tale of Two Minds..., bear witness of how **God's Sovereign Will** *orchestrates the intricate patterns, weaving the threads of our choices, whether good or bad, into the tapestry of HIS DIVINE PURPOSE.*

Jonah and Sharon, are now ordained ministers, and marriage counsellors, spearheading the ministry of:

'LETS MAKE MARRIAGE GREAT AGAIN'

and the humanitarian

"OWECOP MINISTRY"

You can follow and like their pages on **FACEBOOK!**

Jonah and Sharon deeply value the sanctity and sacredness of marriage. Despite their past experiences with divorce from former spouses, they hold fast to the belief in the principle of one spouse for life. Their own divorces do not diminish this core belief.

It's important to clarify that they do not endorse divorce in any way. They recognize that God hates divorce, and they align their views with this biblical teaching. They believe that what God hates, they too should hate.

They understand that opinions on divorce can vary widely, but they emphasize that this Stand is a personal conviction that each individual must discern with God's guidance through the Holy Spirit. The decision on matters of marriage and divorce should ultimately be led by one's relationship with God, seeking His will above all else.

COMING SOON

1. The Bible for Standers:

   Scriptures and Encouragement when believing for the Impossible.

2. 40 Days of Fervent Prayers for your husband.

   AND

3. The Rocky Road to Restoration.

GLOSSARY OF TERMS

Buck – In Caribbean folklore, a buck is a short, dwarf-like creature believed to bring monetary success to those who keep and use it.

Country bookie – A term in Trinidad, used to describe someone who is culturally unlearned or not well-versed, especially if they are from rural areas.

Cut tail – A term referring to a beating administered as punishment for wrongdoing.

Deputy – The "other woman" in a cheating or adulterous relationship.

Dougla – The exact origins of the term "dougla" in Trinidad, referring to the offspring of African-Indian unions, are unclear. Etymologically, the word is linked to an Indic origin, meaning a person of mixed or impure breed. Nevertheless, it is a commonly used term in Trinidadian culture to mean a person of mixed African and East Indian ancestry.

Hard as banga – Referring to someone's unpleasant features or body, with banga being a very hard seed found in the Caribbean.

Hardened – In Trinidad, when someone is described as "hardened," it means they are stubborn and resistant to sound advice.

Herbal tea – In this context, is a concoction similar to a witch's brew, with the intention of casting a spell on the intended victim.

Herbalist doctors – Euphemism for a witch doctors or practitioners of traditional medicine involving herbs and spells.

Obeah – The practice of performing spells and enchantments, often with malicious intent.

Pretty face and "dutty" character – A beautiful woman who engaged in multiple relationships simultaneously, often for financial gain.

Red woman – A woman with lighter skin tone, often stigmatized as a home-wrecker or promiscuous. The term implies a misconception of superiority and being "stuck up." Similarly, "a red man" carries the same perception.

Stink and dutty – A term used in Trinidad to describe scandalous behavior, rather than an actual odor.

Soucouyant (SOO KOO YAH) – A type of shape-shifting, blood-sucking old lady in Caribbean folklore, often seen flying in the night sky as a ball of fire in remote villages.

Sweet looking reds – A beautiful woman with light skin tone, often associated with the stereotype of being a "red woman."

To lime – To socialize and have a gathering with friends/family, usually involving food and (alcoholic) drinks.

The mad house – An unfortunate stereotype suggesting that once a person has been mentally institutionalized, they are deemed permanently insane and incapable of responsibility.

Trini – An abbreviation for a person from Trinidad.

Vegetable – Used in Trinidad to describe a person in a vegetative state, with complete loss of consciousness, limb movement, speech, and ability to follow commands.

Made in the USA
Columbia, SC
08 April 2024

2c6059b5-17b7-4347-9cdf-463c8da5182eR01